50 GEMS

The Black Country

JOHN SHIPLEY

AMBERLEY

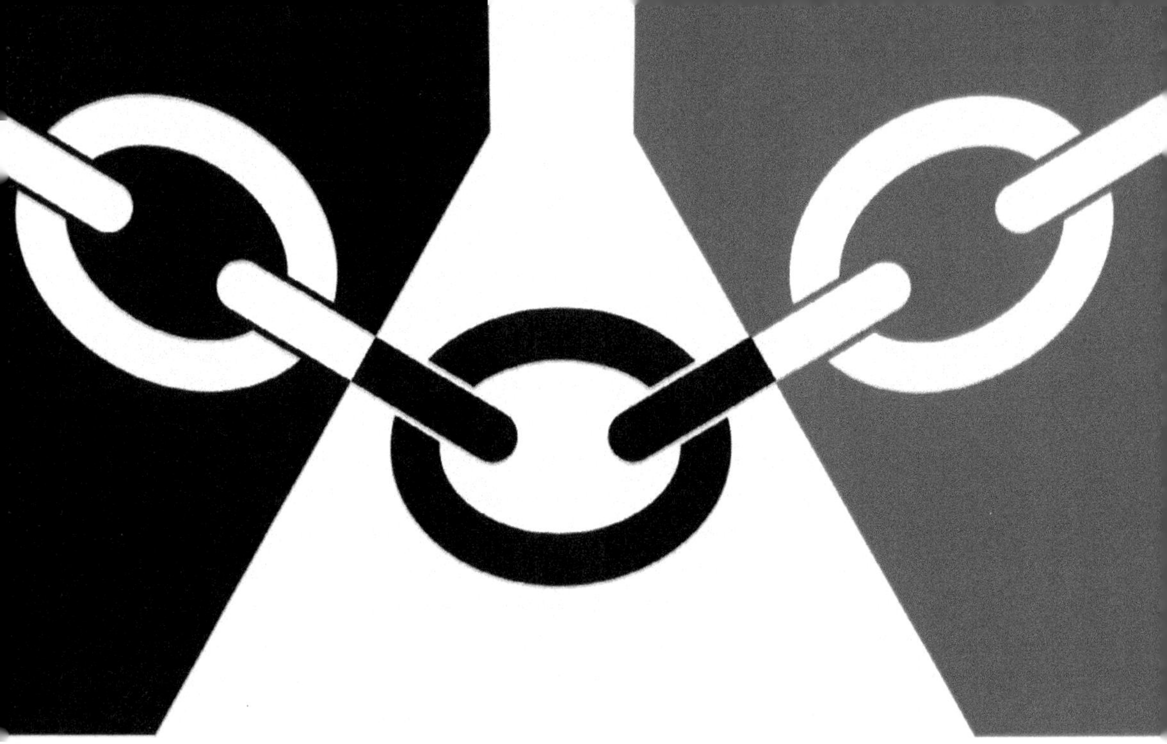

The Black Country flag (designed by Gracie Sheppard).

First published 2019

Amberley Publishing
The Hill, Stroud
Gloucestershire, GL5 4EP

www.amberley-books.com

British Library Cataloguing in Publication Data.
A catalogue record for this book is available from the British Library.

ISBN 978 1 4456 9416 0 (paperback)
ISBN 978 1 4456 9417 7 (ebook)

Typesetting by Aura Technology and Software Services, India.
Printed in Great Britain.

Contents

Map 5
Introduction 6

The Dudley Metropolitan Borough Area 9
1. The Black Country Living Museum, Dudley 9
2. Dudley Canal Trust and Wren's Nest Caverns 12
3. Dudley Castle and Dudley Zoological Gardens 17
4. Dudley Priory 20
5. Stourbridge Glass Quarter 22
6. Halesowen Abbey 23
7. Holbeche House, Kingswinford, Hagley Hall, Near Stourbridge, and the Gunpowder Plot 25
8. Saltwells Nature Reserve 28
9. Mushroom Green, Netherton 29
10. The Crooked House – The Glynne Arms 31
11. Barrow Hill Nature Reserve and Pensnett Volcano 32
12. The Fountain Inn and the Tipton Slasher 33
13. Cotwall End Country Park 35
14. Wychbury Ring, Near Stourbridge 36
15. Himley Hall and Park 37
16. The Leasowes 38

The Sandwell Metropolitan Borough Area 40
17. The Oak House, West Bromwich 40
18. Sandwell Valley Country Park, Sandwell Priory, Priory Woods Local Nature Reserve, Sandwell Park Farm and Sot's Hole Nature Reserve 41
19. The Manor House, West Bromwich 45
20. Sheepwash Urban Park, Horseley Heath 46
21. Steward Aqueduct, Smethwick 47
22. Engine Arm Aqueduct, Smethwick 49
23. Ethelfleda Terrace and St Bartholemew's Church, Wednesbury 50
24. Ye Olde Leathern Bottel, Wednesbury 53
25. Cobb's Engine House, Warren Hall Local Nature Reserve and Bumble Hole Local Nature Reserve 54
26. Bishop Asbury Cottage, Great Barr 57
27. Haden Hill House and Park, Cradley Heath 58
28. Corngreaves Hall and Corngreaves Nature Reserve 60
29. Warley Woods Park 61
30. The Hawthorns, Home of West Bromwich Albion 62

The Wolverhampton Metropolitan Borough Area 63
31. Bantock House and Park, Wolverhampton 63
32. Molineux, Home of Wolverhampton Wanderers 65
33. Moseley Old Hall, Wolverhampton, and the Monarch's Way 67
34. Northycote Farm and Country Park, Bushbury, Wolverhampton 73
35. Wightwick Manor, Compton 74

36. Wolverhampton's Twenty-one Locks 75
37. Sedgley Beacon Tower 76
38. St Wulfuna's Cross, St Peter's Church, Wolverhampton, and St Wulfruna's Well 77
39. Lady Godiva's Cross and St Bartholemew's Church, Upper Penn 81
40. The Grand Theatre, Wolverhampton 83

The Walsall Metropolitan Borough Area 85
41. Barr Beacon 85
42. Moorcroft Wood Nature Reserve, Moxley 87
43. Great Barr Hall and Park 87
44. Rushall Hall 88
45. Castle Old Fort, Stonnall 89
46. Rough Wood Country Park, Short Heath 90
47. The White Hart, Caldmore, Walsall 91
48. Shire Oak Park Nature Reserve 92
49. Walsall Leather Museum 93
50. Walsall Arboretum 94

Postscript 95
Acknowledgements 95
About the Author 96

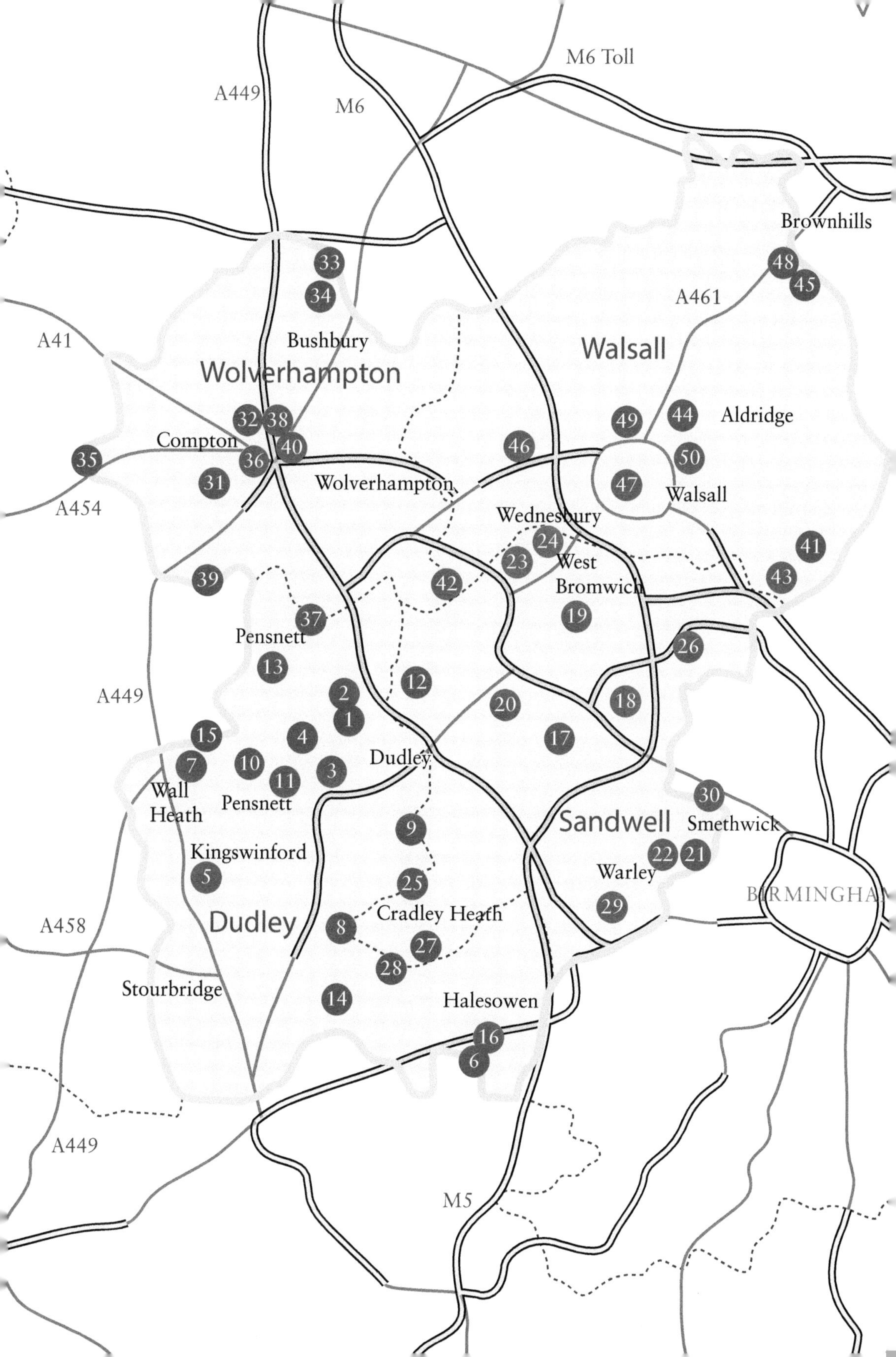
M6 Toll
A449
M6
Brownhills
A461
Walsall
A41
Bushbury
Wolverhampton
Aldridge
Compton
Wolverhampton
Walsall
A454
Wednesbury
West
Bromwich
Pensnett
A449
Dudley
Wall
Heath
Pensnett
Sandwell
Smethwick
Kingswinford
Warley
BIRMINGHA
Cradley Heath
Dudley
A458
Stourbridge
Halesowen
A449
M5
33
34
32
38
40
36
35
31
39
37
13
2
1
12
42
23
24
46
49
44
50
47
48
45
41
43
19
26
18
20
17
15
7
10
11
4
3
9
25
8
27
28
14
16
6
30
22
21
29
5

Introduction

Welcome to *50 Gems of the Black Country*. Let's start by attempting to define what constitutes the area known as the Black Country. The traditional notion is that the Black Country consists of those parts of South Staffordshire and North Worcestershire under which lays the famous 30-foot seam of coal. The Black Country Society states that the traditional Black Country towns (in alphabetical order) are Bilston, Blackheath, Coseley, Cradley Heath, Dudley, parts of Halesowen, Oldbury, Old Hill, Smethwick/Warley, Tipton, parts of Walsall, parts of Wednesbury, Wednesfield, West Bromwich, and Wolverhampton.

Today the Black Country is spread over the four Metropolitan District Councils of Dudley, Sandwell, Walsall, and Wolverhampton, a total physical area of around 138 square miles (360 square kilometres), and this is the area and its places that I have described in this book. So to the earlier mentioned list we can add the following: Aldridge, Amblecote, Bloxwich, Bradley, Brierley Hill, Brownhills, Bushbury, Cradley, Darlaston, Dudley Port, Ettingshall, Great Barr, Great Bridge, Hagley, Kingswinford, Lye, Moxley, Netherton, Pelsall, Pensnett, Quarry Bank, Rowley Regis, Rushall, Sedgley, Stourbridge, Upper and Lower Gornal, and Wombourne.

However, in reality the Black Country has no single set of defined boundaries or border. For me the Black Country is more of a cultural boundary than anything geographical. So as far as I'm concerned, 'if yo think yo'me from the Black Country then yo am!'

In 1863, the American Consul to Birmingham, a man by the name of Elihu Burritt, reputedly wrote that the area was 'Black by day, and red by night'. Burritt wrote three travel books about Britain. His third, *Walks in The Black Country and its Green Borderland*, published in 1868, brought the Black Country name to prominence. American diplomat Burritt had been appointed by Abraham Lincoln in 1862 to the office of first US Consul to Birmingham.

By around 1860 in the Black Country there were over 400 mining pits, more than 180 blast furnaces, plus 118 ironworks, seventy-nine rolling mills and 1,500 puddling furnaces, every one of them spewing out smoke. Reputedly Queen Victoria loathed the area so much that when her royal train passed through she insisted on the curtains in her carriage being closed.

So where did the name come from? Here you can choose your own version. In his diary entry for 22 July 1834, prominent English actor Charles Mayne Young compared a Lincolnshire village with the densely populated Black Country with its smoke and blasts and furnaces. Young's diary was published in 1871 and his subsequent additions cast doubt on the originality of his 1834 diary entry. Prior to this the term had been applied to an area on the Belgian border, centred around

Charleroi, known as Pays-Noir, as well as to Ethiopia and Sudan. An earlier mention came from the Lichfield town clerk Mr Simpson, addressing a reformers meeting on 24 November 1841. He described going into the black country of Staffordshire – Wolverhampton, Bilston and Tipton – and an account of this was published in the *Staffordshire Advertiser*. Then there was Revd William Gresley, prebendary of Lichfield Cathedral, who used the term in his novel *Colton Green: A Tale of the Black Country*, published in 1846. The term appeared again in an 1849 article in the *London Illustrated News*, and in the 1851 guidebook to the London and North Western Railway, plus loads more, too numerous to mention.

Black Country Day is 14 July, and the Black Country flag was designed by Stourbridge schoolgirl Gracie Sheppard of Redhill School, in a competition that she won in 2012.

We have the Black Country Society and the Black Country Bugle to thank for promoting the area and for keeping its traditions alive and in the public eye. Not forgetting those traditional mythical comedic characters 'Anock and Ali' (Enoch and Eli), played for years by John Plant and Alan Smith. Now we have the long-running *Black Country Night Out* show originally featuring Harry Harrison, Dolly Allen and that great comedian Tommy Mundon, now with my mates Alan and Glynnis Briscoe, better known as Dandy.

I was born in 1942, during the Second World War, in the home of my maternal grandparents at No. 26 Pound Road, Wednesbury. I attended Lower High Street Infant's School, Holyhead Road Boy's Senior School (Woden County Secondary Modern), and Wednesbury Technical College, where I later attended night school and day release from my job as an apprentice draughtsman at the Patent Shaft & Axletree Company Ltd, Wednesbury, renamed the Patent Shaft Steel Works in 1959. My dad, my granddad and a couple of uncles also worked there.

When I was a lad I remember sitting on Ethelfleda Terrace on Church Hill after school with my mates peering in awe through the murky smoke towards Dudley Castle, which was high on a dark distant hill on the horizon, firing our imaginations that we were medieval knights. The castle was only around 5 miles away, but to me it seemed much further. As I gazed I was amazed by the wondrous explosions that illuminated the skyline as, one by one, furnaces were tapped – each sending an explosion of colour skywards – vivid reds, yellows and oranges, dazzlingly bright against the otherwise dark and murky landscape. Most days you couldn't see the castle through the murk. The smoke-filled atmosphere had a distinct smell of its own, a kind of pungent coke (the kind you burn) aroma. My dad told me that the reason we didn't need an alarm clock was because the early morning coughs of the sparrows woke us up. Then there was the eerie wail of the various bulls (sirens) that pierced the air, informing workers that one shift was ending and another was about to begin. Each compelled armies of men and women to their place of employment for another eight hours of hot and sweaty toil. These folks certainly earned their corn. It's so different today – no smoke, no smog, no sparrows coughing their little hearts out.

Industrial expansion in Victorian times and beyond exploited the West Midlands countryside. The construction of those dark satanic mills and factories, and the need for cheap terraced housing for the workers who flocked from all around the British Isles and further afield to find work caused the destruction of far too many historic buildings. In those days there was no place for the quaint and spacious. Terraced houses were crammed in among the myriad of factories, large and small, that sprang up. And so the leisurely picturesque villages and village greens mostly disappeared from the landscape, replaced by fast-moving places of manufacture and toil.

During my time at the Patent Shaft I got to design and draw a huge variety of things, including the Patent Shaft Steel Works logo – PSSW – and the metal gates that stood at each entrance to the works. Although the Shaft is no longer around, one set of those gates stand proudly on the traffic island at the intersection of the Holyhead Road and Leabrook Road, in Wednesbury, near the bus station and fire station. The gates were recovered and originally sited on Patent Way before being refurbished and moved to their present location. Living in Bridgnorth, I don't get to see these gates very often but each time I do I get a great feeling of pride to think something I designed is still standing.

The Black Country is in the hearts and minds of the people who live there, and still is for those like my wife and I who have moved away. Today, we live in Bridgnorth, a place where my family used to sometimes go on their summer holidays.

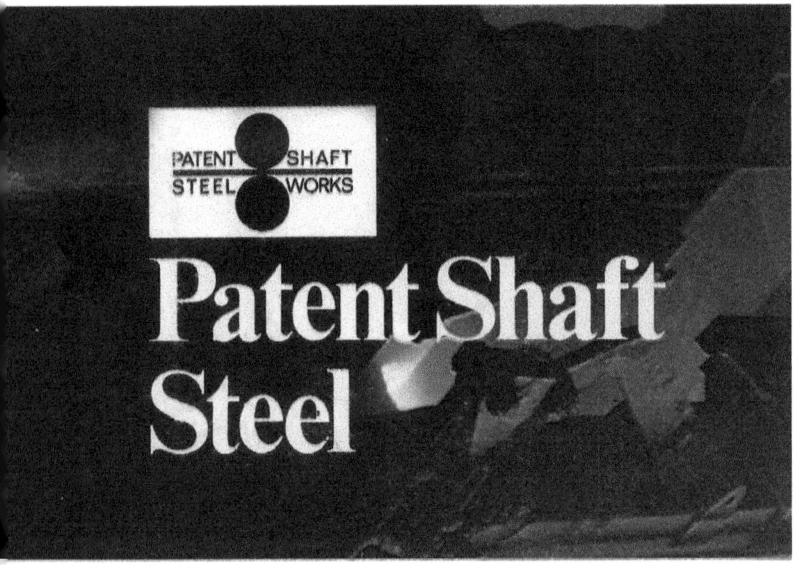

Left: Patent Shaft Steel Works logo.

Below: The Patent Shaft gates.

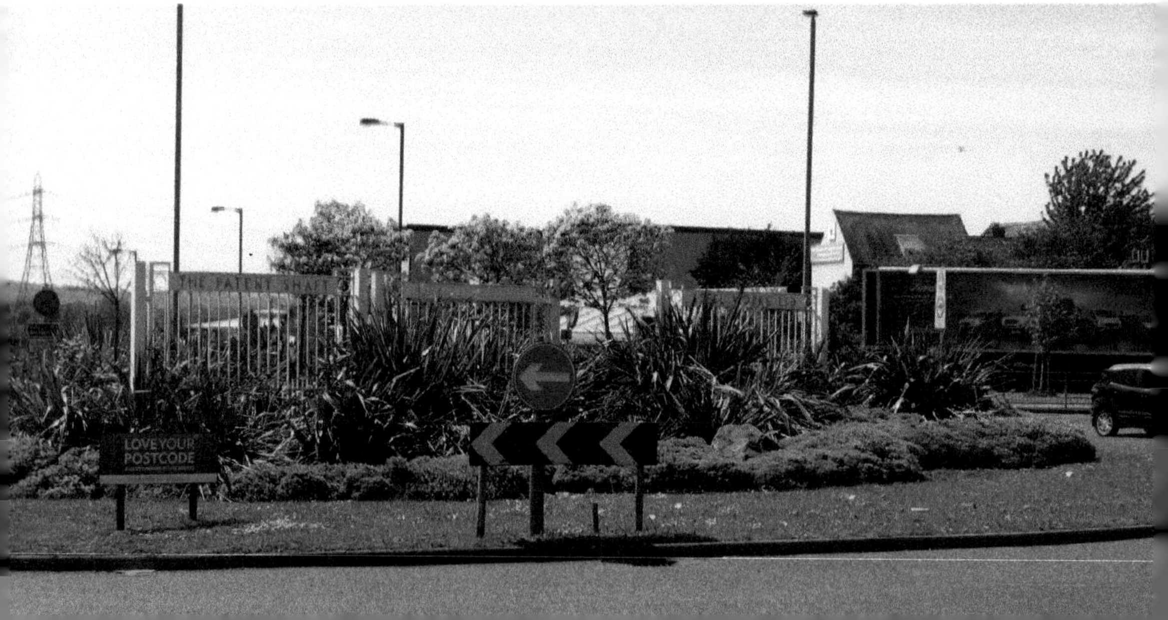

The Dudley Metropolitan Borough Area

The settlement that later became known as Dudley was, in Anglo-Saxon times, called Dudda's or Duddan's Leigh, which translates to 'Dudda's or Duddan's Clearing' in Old English; in other words, land worked by a guy called Dudda, with 'leigh' meaning a 'wooded clearing'. Unfortunately, history does not tell us anything about this man. There are claims that he was Dodo or Doddo, a Mercian nobleman, and that he constructed a fortification there around AD 700.

Prior to the arrival of the Normans, the town was owned by Earl Edwin of Mercia, brother-in-law to King Harold I (Godwinson). The 1086 Domesday Book lists Dudelei as being in the Hundred of Clent (funny that's how a lot of local folk pronounce the town's name today).

Sometimes called 'The Capital of the Black Country', a title hotly disputed by other towns in the area, the Metropolitan Borough of Dudley was created in 1974, consisting of Dudley, Stourbridge, Halesowen, Brierley Hill, Sedgley, Amblecote, Rowley Regis and parts of Coseley.

1. The Black Country Living Museum

The attraction that in my opinion best embodies the spirit of the Black Country is the Black Country Living Museum, which is closely associated with the Dudley Canal Trust and Wren's Nest Caverns.

It was way back in the 1950s that the notion of creating a museum of the Black Country was first floated, but it wasn't until 1966 that the idea finally came to fruition when Dudley Metropolitan Borough Council set up the museum department. In 1976 the museum parted company with Dudley Council, and on a tract of derelict land adjacent to the A4037 the museum was born. The site included a canal, a water treatment plant and several old mine shafts. In 1980 a tramway system was added, and in 1990 the underground mine experience opened. And so from humble beginnings

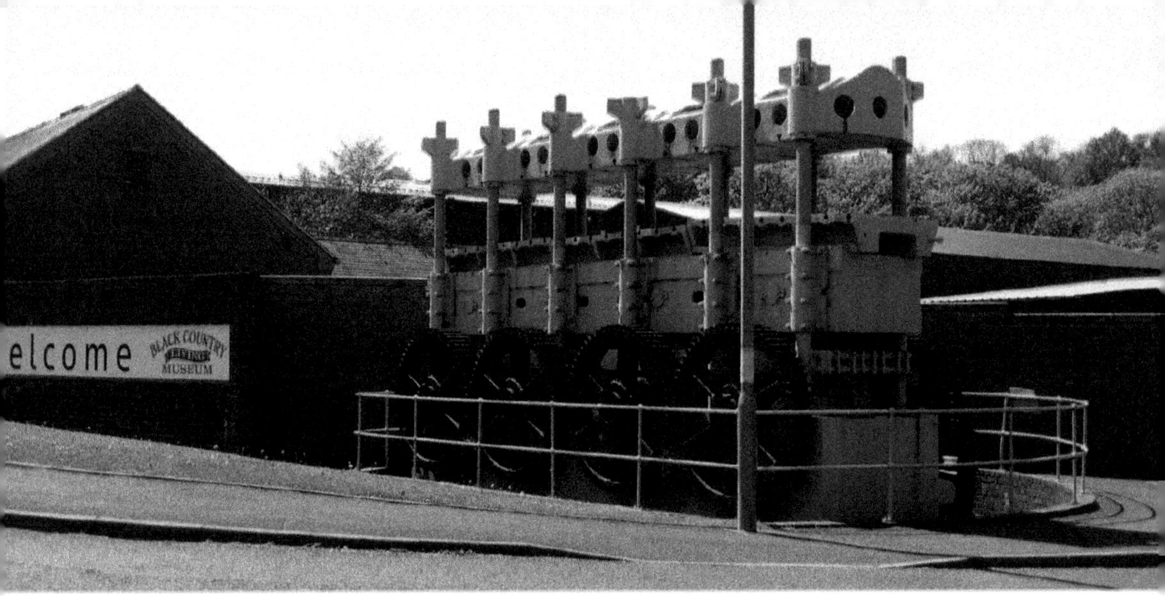

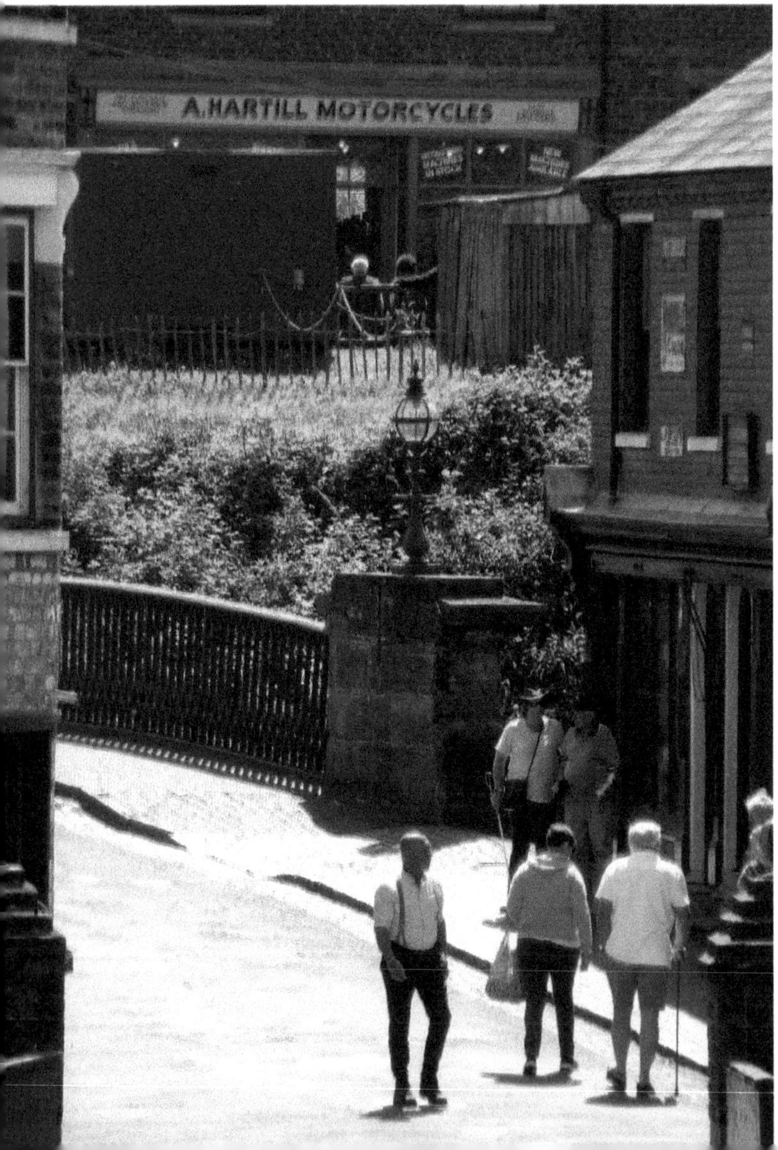

Above: The Black Country Living Museum.

Left: Canal Street, Black Country Living Museum.

the number and scale of exhibits expanded every year, resulting in the wonderful open-air museum we see today. In 2010 the museum welcomed its 7 millionth visitor, and in 2012 the museum was awarded Designation by the Arts Council of England.

There's something for everyone: two mine shafts – go underground and experience what it was like for miners in the nineteenth century; limekilns, canal arm and boat dock; have a drink in the Bottle & Glass Inn – a real Black Country spit and sawdust pub; enjoy some traditional fish and chips cooked in beef drippin'; watch a silent film in the 1921 Limelight Cinema; see how chains and nails are made, and see the brass foundry; go back to school for an old time lesson; take a ride on a tram, bus or trolleybus; play traditional children's games; and enjoy the traditional funfair. Or just stroll around cobbled Stone Street where historic buildings have been relocated to create a canal-side village.

The museum is the location for many television and film shoots including *Peaky Blinders* and *Stan and Ollie*.

Address: Tipton Road, Dudley, DY1 4SQ. Tel: 0121 557 9643. E-mail: info@bclm.com.

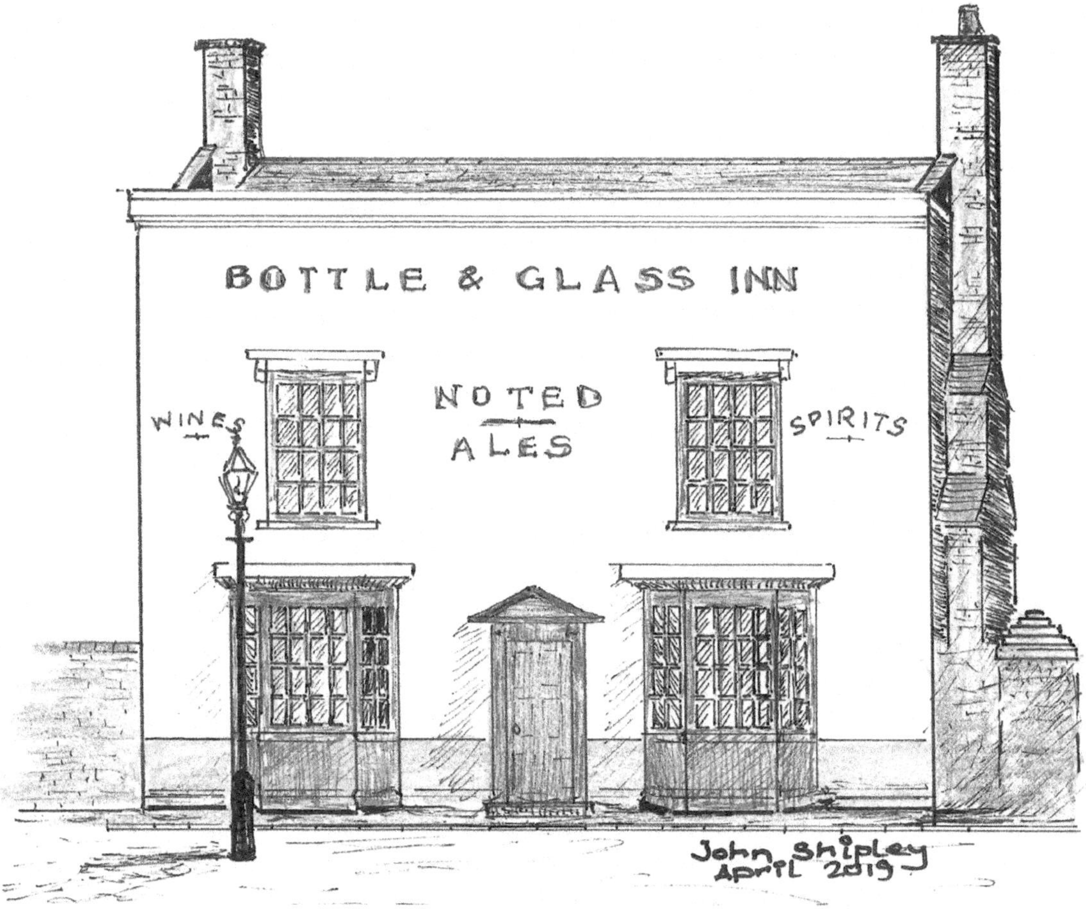

The Bottle & Glass Inn, Black Country Museum. (Pen and ink drawing by John Shipley)

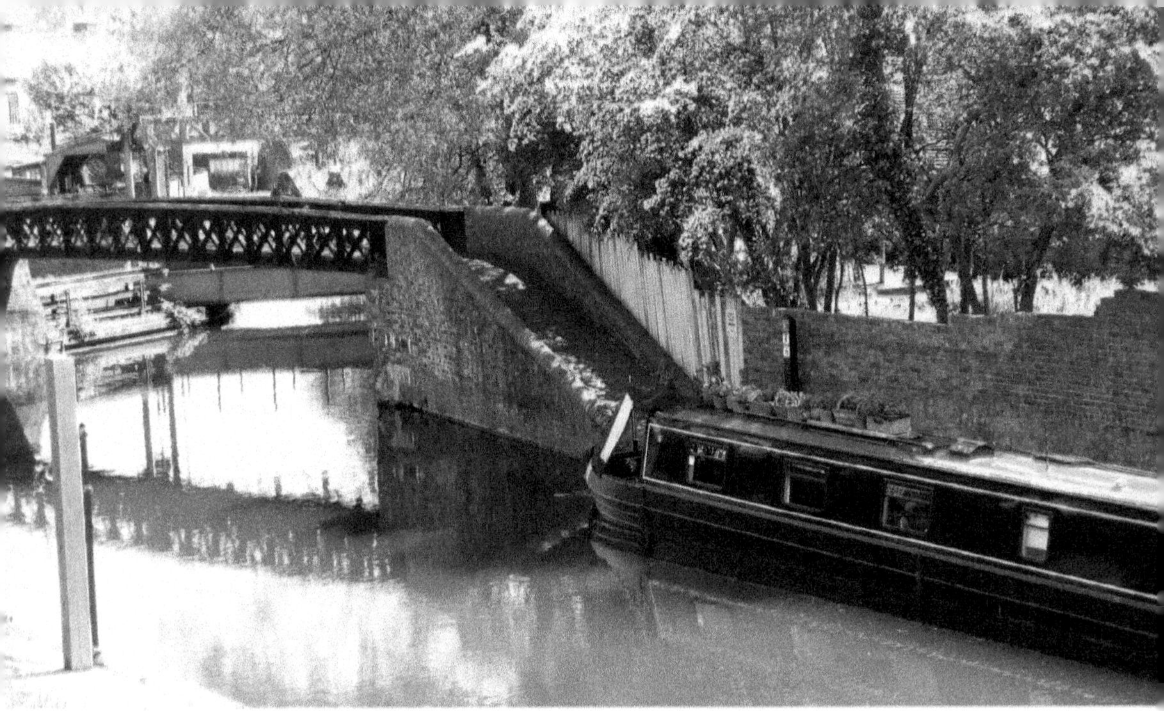

Canal basin, Black Country Living Museum.

2. Dudley Canal Trust (Formerly the Dudley Canal Tunnel Restoration Society) and Wren's Nest Caverns

Operated by the Dudley Canal Charitable Trust, the Dudley Tunnel is situated on the Dudley Canal Line No 1. At around 3,172 yards (2,900.5 metres) long, it's arguably the second longest canal tunnel in the UK – this is sometimes disputed because the tunnel has three sections, i.e. it's not continuous. The first section, Lord Ward's Tunnel at 196 yards (179.2 metres) long, leads to Shirts Mill Basin. The second leading to Castle Mill Basin is a mere 34 yards (31.1 metres) long. The third is Main Dudley Canal Tunnel, at 2,942 yards (2,690.2 metres) long.

Work to construct the tunnel began in 1775 and was completed in 1791. Designed to link Lord Dudley's (John Ward, 2nd Viscount Dudley and Ward) Tipton colliery to the Birmingham Canal Navigations, early in its construction it was also used for the transportation of limestone from the mines below Castle Hill. From Castle Mill Basin the main tunnel runs through the spectacular Cathedral Arch to Parkhead near Netherton. A separate branch, now blocked, once led to the Little Tess Cavern mine workings.

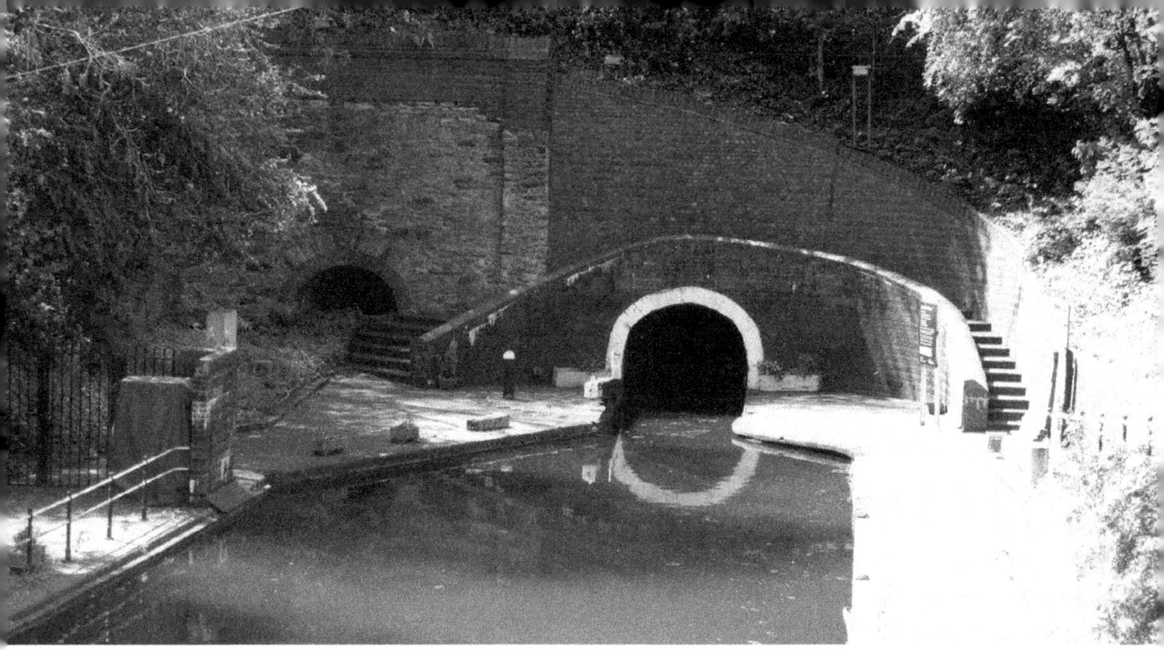

Entrance to Lord Ward's Tunnel.

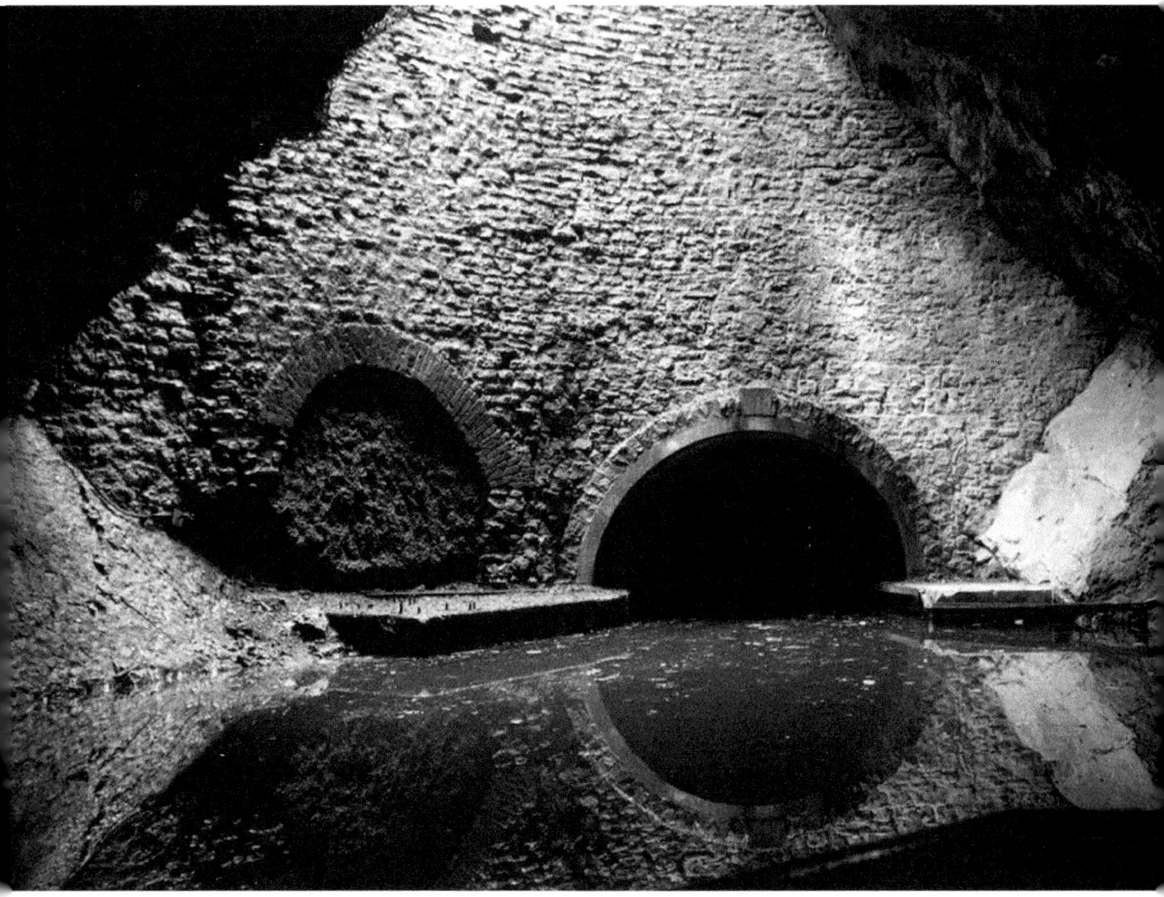

Inside the Dudley Tunnel. (Courtesy of Phil Wild)

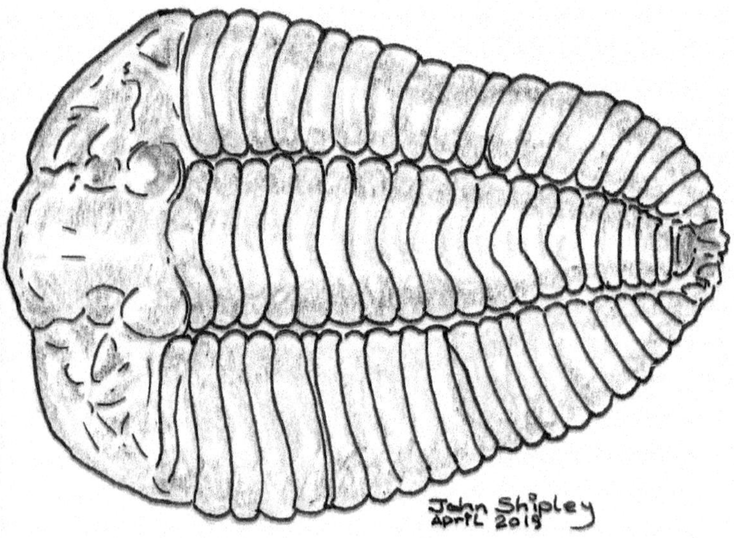

Calymene blumenbachii (the Dudley Bug). (Pen and ink drawing by John Shipley)

The Dudley Tunnel was closed in 1962, but reopened in 1973 following extensive restoration. Two new tunnels were constructed in 1989 linking the wonderfully named Singing Cavern and the Rock Tunnel to Castle Mill Basin via the Little Tess Cavern.

The tunnel is too narrow for some boats and of course there is no towpath. Also the absence of ventilation prohibits the use of diesel engines, so the only way to move a barge forward is to 'leg it', or to take a trip on the trust's battery-powered barges. The practice of 'legging' requires one to lie on ones back on the roof of the barge and literally walk along the underside of the tunnel roof or walls. The Oolitic limestone through which the tunnels were dug is packed with Trilobite fossils. The best is a Calymene blumenbachii, known as the Dudley Bug.

If it's picturesque sights you want you won't find any better than Wren's Nest with its caverns under Castle Hill, Dudley, a Site of Special Scientific Interest. This important geological site is a well-preserved example of a Silurian Coral Reef, which includes many wide-ranging fossils. It's also a nature reserve and home to many species of birds, bats, and rare flora.

Wren's Nest's most famous son, Abraham Darby, one of the founding fathers of the historic Industrial Revolution, was born here in 1678.

The caverns were mined for limestone, initially used for mortar and in agriculture, and later in the iron production process; reputedly at its zenith 20,000 tons were dug out each year. Quarrying ceased and the site was abandoned around 1925.

Sadly major roof collapses and cave-ins in 2001 forced the Severn Sisters Tunnel complex to be closed, and today there is limited access. The Dudley Canal & Tunnel trust offer a number of different tours starting from Portal Building Visitor Centre accessed independently or via the Black Country Living Museum. Check out their website for details: www.dudleycanaltrust.org.uk.

Address: Dudley Canal & Tunnel Trust, Portal Centre, Birmingham New Road, Dudley, DY1 4SB.

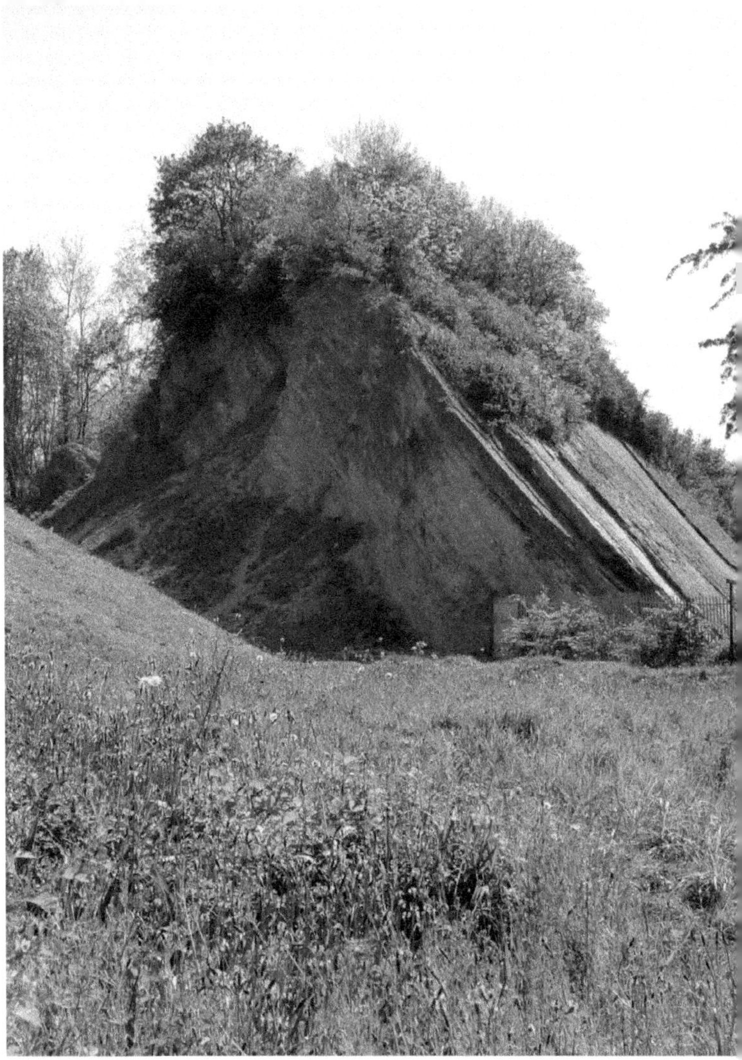

Right and below: Wren's Nest Nature Reserve.

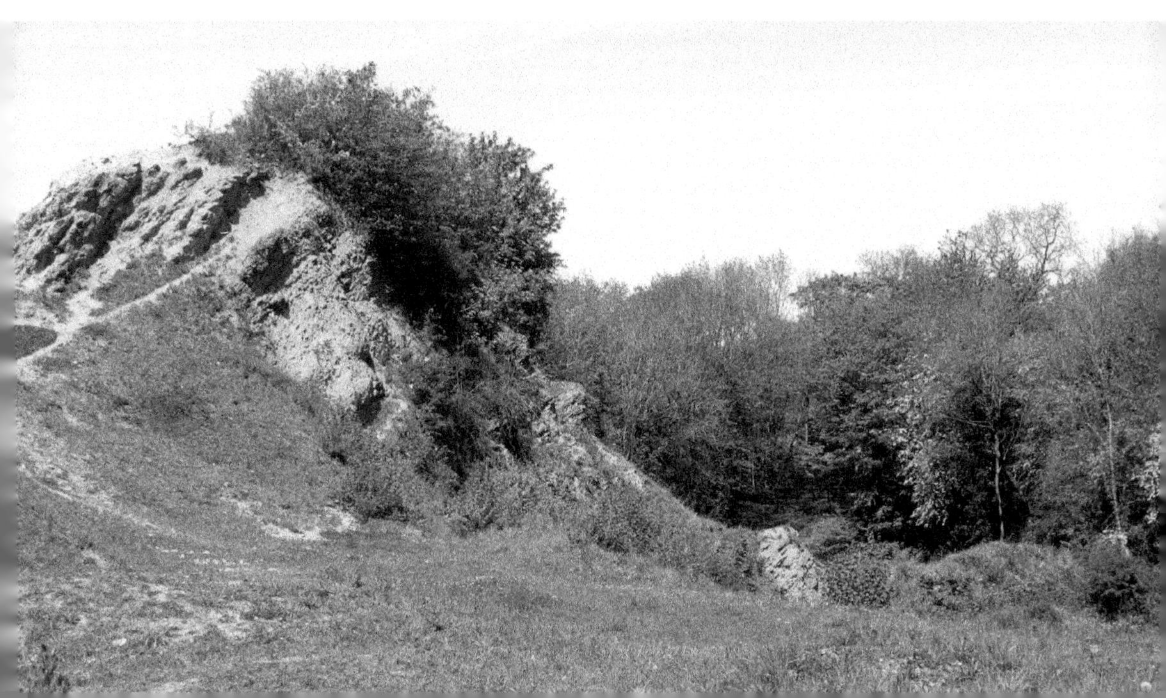

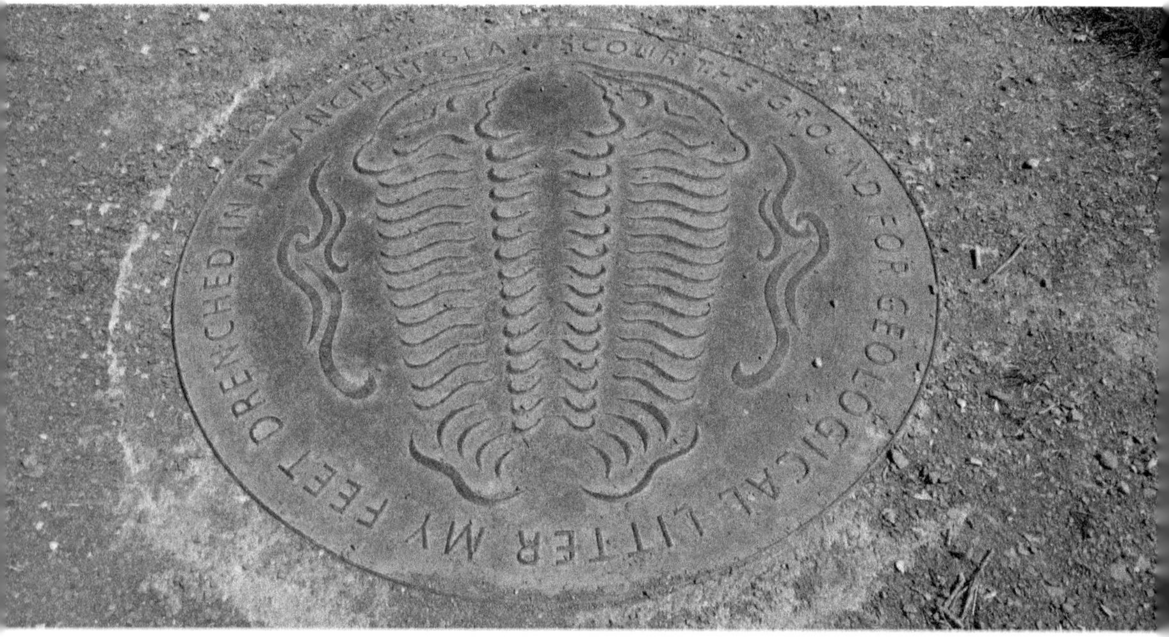

Dudley Bug tablet, Wren's Nest Nature Reserve.

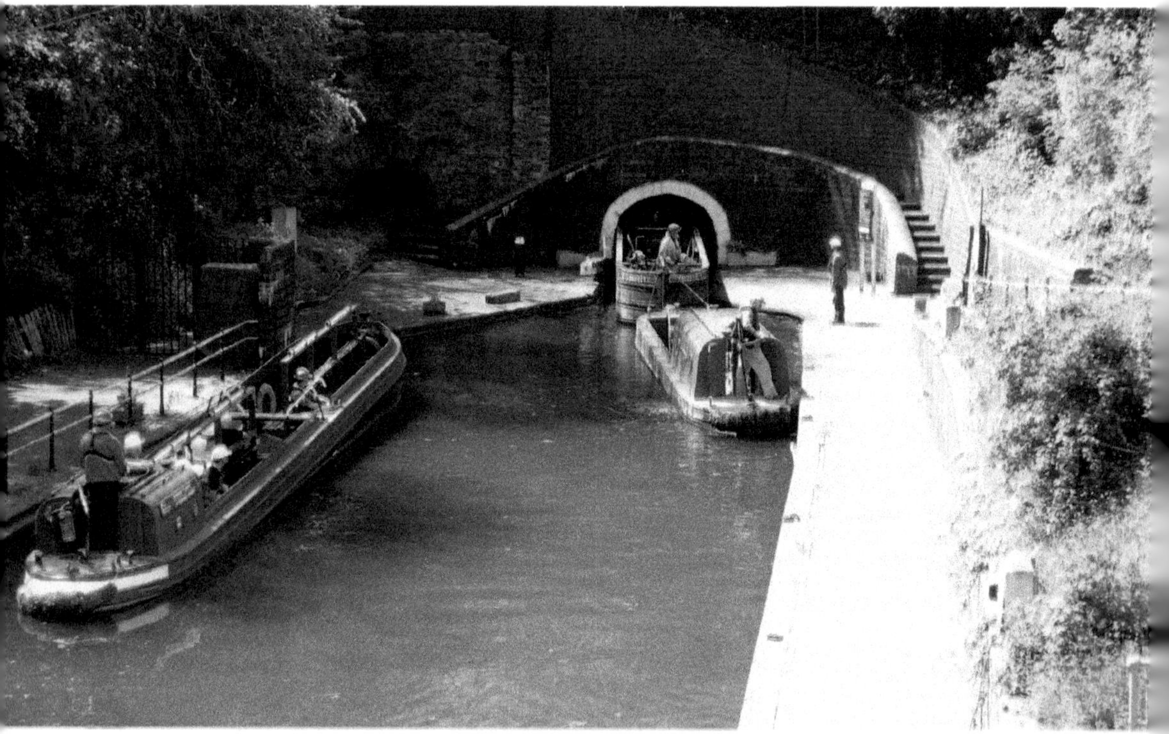

Canal boat trips.

3. Dudley Castle and Dudley Zoological Gardens

Dudley Castle was built in 1070, a few years after the 1066 Norman invasion, by Ansculf de Picquigny, a Norman baron from the town of Picquiny, near Amiens in Picardy, who came over to England as part of William the Conquerer's invasion. Ansculf must have done well because Duke William rewarded him with eighty manors. The 1086 Domesday Book lists the town as being owned by Ansculf's son and heir William Fitz-Ansculf (Fitz meaning son of).

The original castle would have been a traditional Norman timber motte-and-bailey. The stone castle replacement was erected in the twelfth century by the Paganell family. In 1173 the castle was demolished by order of Henry II. Rebuilding began in the latter part of the thirteenth century using limestone and sandstone by Roger de Somery II, and work continued into the fourteenth century by Roger's descendants.

Over the centuries the castle has been the scene of much conflict. Sixty-nine years after the death of William I (William the Conqueror), the country was in the grip of a civil war (known as the Anarchy) lasting from 1135 to 1153. The Earl of Dudley supported the claims of Empress Matilda, the Conqueror's granddaughter and his chosen heir, against the claims of her cousin King Stephen. Stephen attacked and besieged the castle in 1138.

Dudley Castle. (Courtesy of Phil Wild)

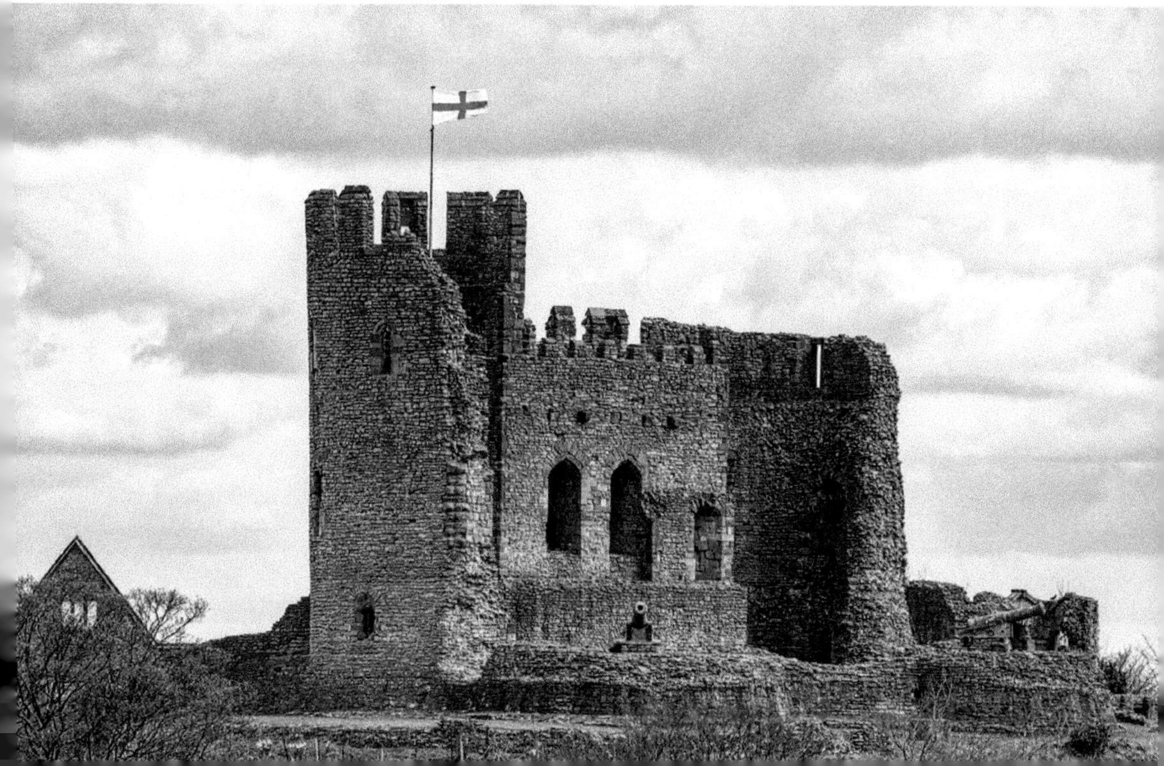

Ownership of the castle passed from the de Somery's to the de Suttons, and then to John Dudley, later Duke of Northumberland and great-grandson of John Sutton, 1st Baron Dudley. Building work continued and a new sumptuous three-storey range of buildings, incorporating a great hall, kitchen, servery, buttery, cellars and bedrooms, was erected within the old walls, described as being one of the earliest examples of Italian Renaissance influenced architecture in the area. In 1533 John Dudley was executed for his involvement in the attempt to install Lady Jane Grey as Queen of England.

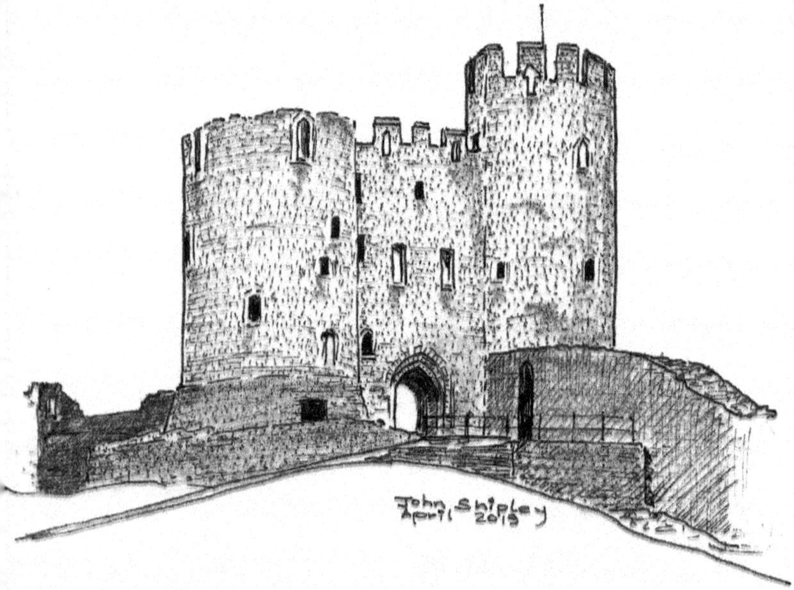

Left: The ruins of Dudley Castle keep. (Pen and ink drawing by John Shipley)

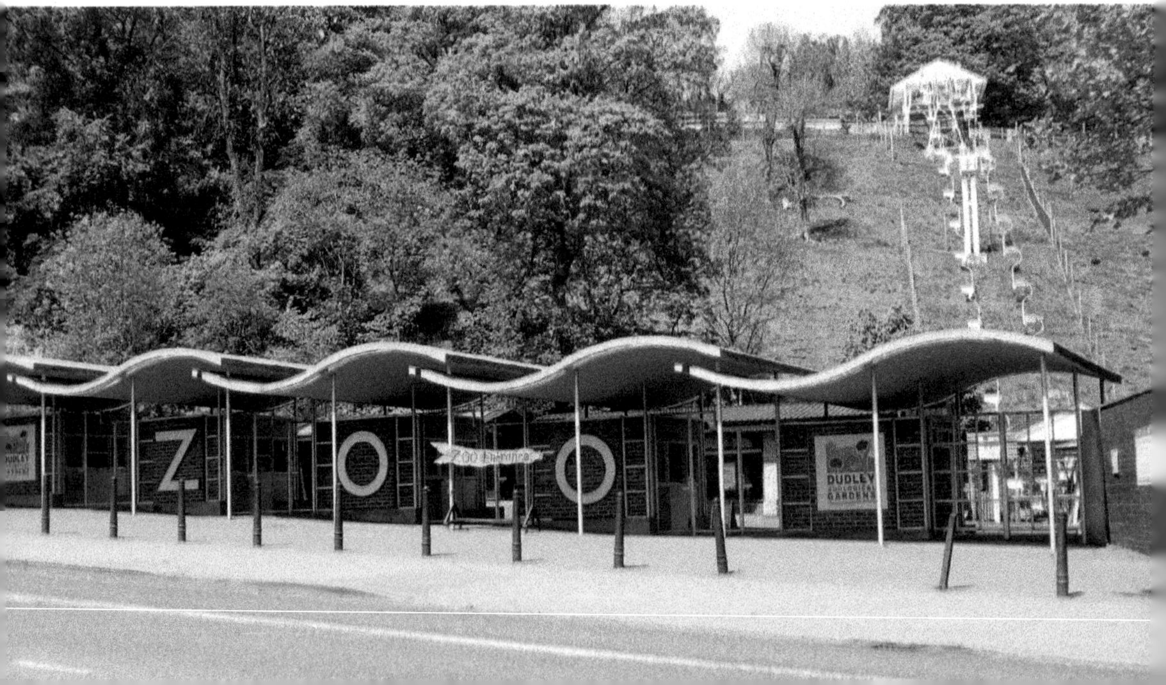

Below: Dudley Zoo's iconic entrance.

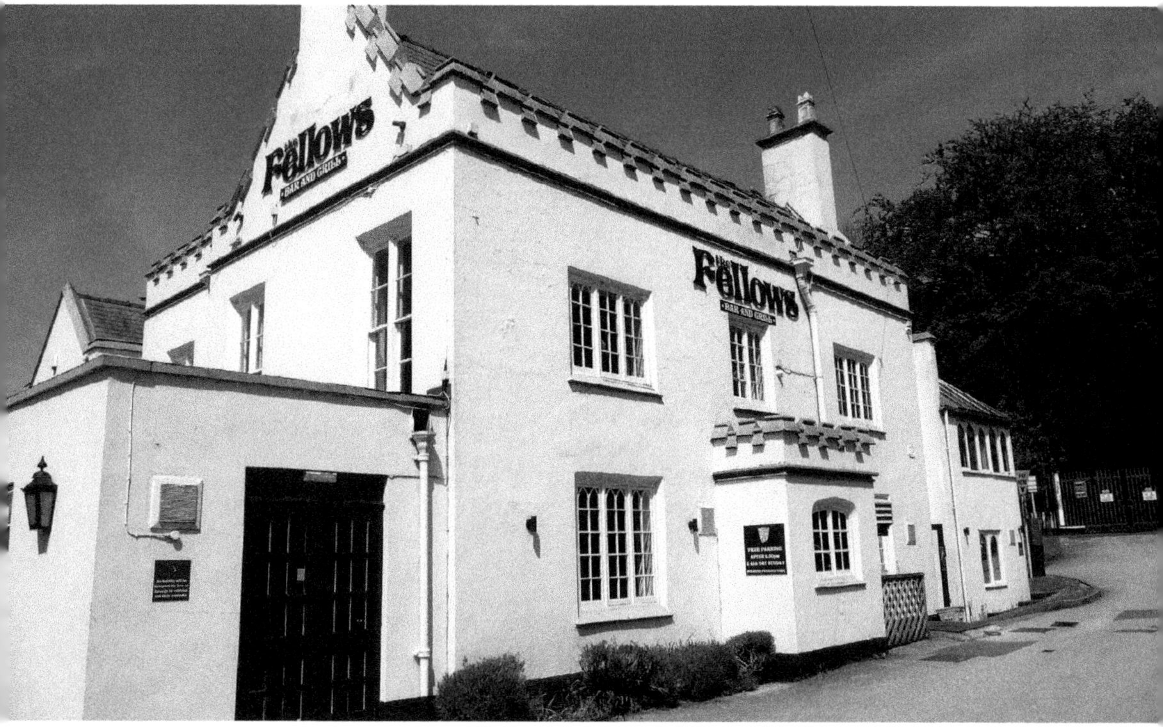

The Fellows landmark pub, Dudley, once the Fellows Club, meeting place of the Fellows of the Dudley Zoological Society from 1937 to the mid-1960s.

During the First English Civil War the castle was garrisoned for Charles I and commanded by Colonel Thomas Leveson. The Roundheads laid siege twice, the second time under Sir William Brereton, capturing the castle on 13 May 1646, and the order was given to slight the castle fortifications. Despite being part demolished the Earls of Dudley continued to occasionally reside here, although it's reported that they much preferred to live in Himley Hall. In 1750 a great fire turned this once beautiful fortification into an uninhabitable ruin.

The castle was converted into a zoo in 1937 by the Earl of Dudley, with buildings designed by Berthold Lubetkin using limestone and reddish sandstone.

The shell of the fourteenth-century oblong-shaped keep with semicircular drum towers at angles, together with the barbican and curtain walls are still standing, as is the sixteenth-century great hall with the remains of eight-light transomed mullions, also the chapel and undercroft.

Dudley Zoological Gardens are better known as Dudley Zoo. I wish I had a tenner for every time I've been there! In the 1960s my band played a number of times at the Queen Mary Ballroom in the zoo, and I recall how scary it was packing up after midnight. Outside in the pitch dark, the scents, sounds and grunts of the animals was like being on safari in Africa. On the plus side there was always a good crowd at the dances. Check out the website for details of the extensive attractions. The zoo opened to visitors in 1937.

Address: Castle Hill, Dudley, DY1 4QF. Website: www.dudleyzoo.org.uk.

4. Dudley Priory

Sadly only part of the shell, footings and foundations, plus a few other features of this Grade I listed building, remain. It was founded in 1160 by Gervase Paganell as a dependency of the Cluniac Priory at Much Wenlock, following the traditions of Cluny Abbey in France. Dedicated to St James and built using limestone mined on Wren's Nest, the priory church became the burial place of the Lords of Dudley. The priory was in effect part-moated with large fishponds and a mill pond located on three of its sides. Extended and enhanced over the thirteenth, fourteenth and fifteenth centuries the priory thrived until Henry VIII's Dissolution of the Monasteries which took place between 1536 and 1541. In *c.* 1545 the estates were granted to Sir John Dudley, 1st Duke of Northumberland, however, following his execution for treason, the priory buildings fell into ruin.

The priory ruins can be found in Priory Park, a 19-acre (7.7-ha) public open space, which opened in 1932. Also situated in the park is Priory Hall, a Grade II listed Tudor-style Ashlar building built in 1825 by the Earl of Dudley. This hall is now home to the Dudley Register Office. The earlier ponds were drained when the hall was built.

Address: Priory Park, No. 23 Paganel Drive, off The Broadway (A459), Dudley, DY1 4AZ.

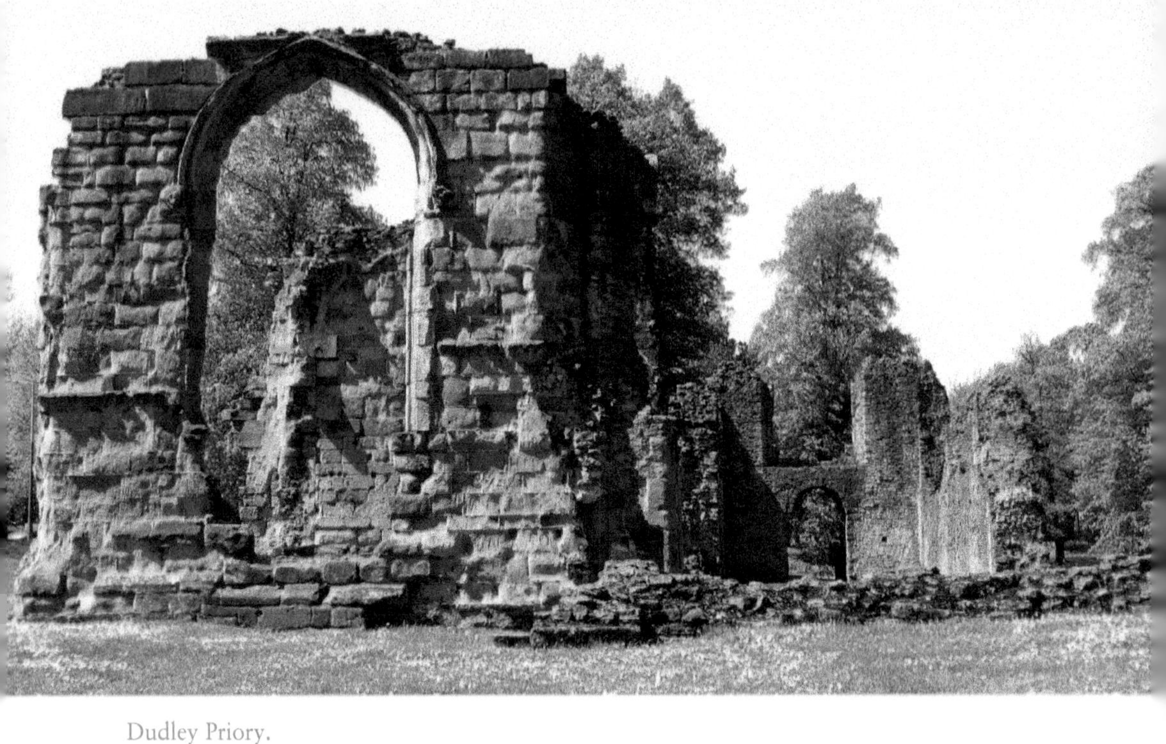

Dudley Priory.

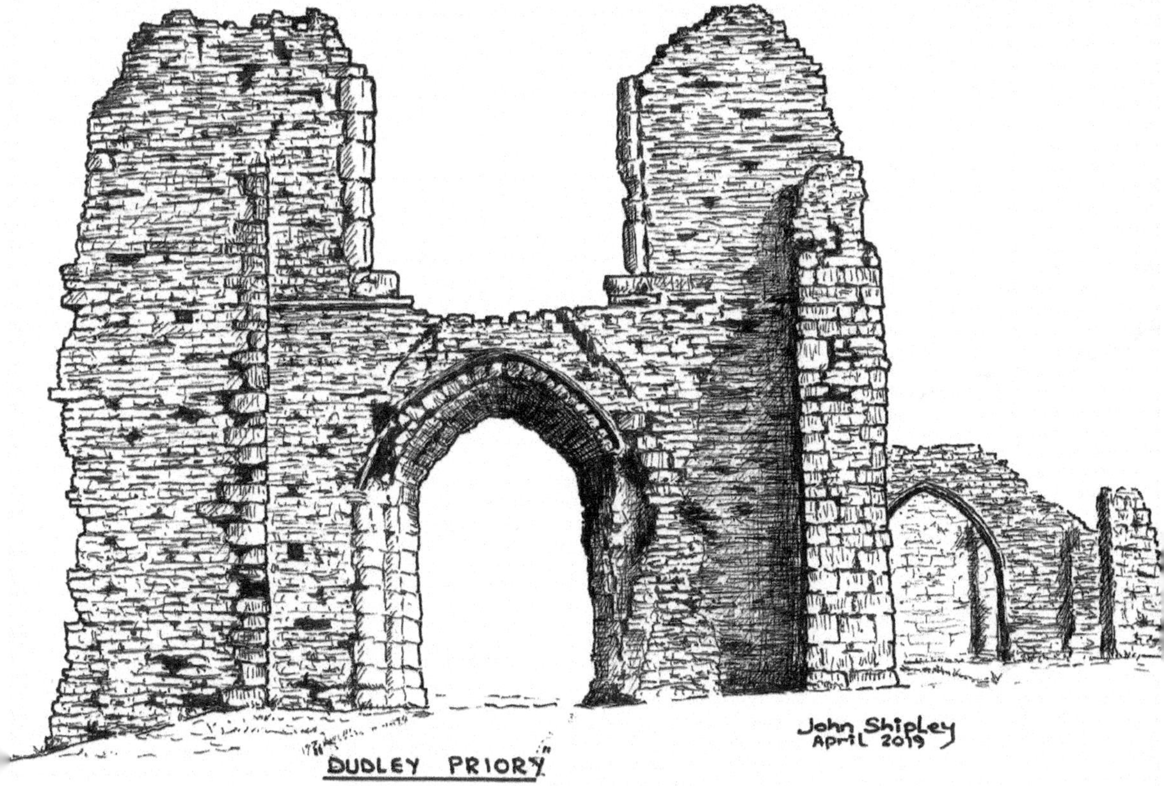

Dudley Priory. (Pen and ink drawing by John Shipley)

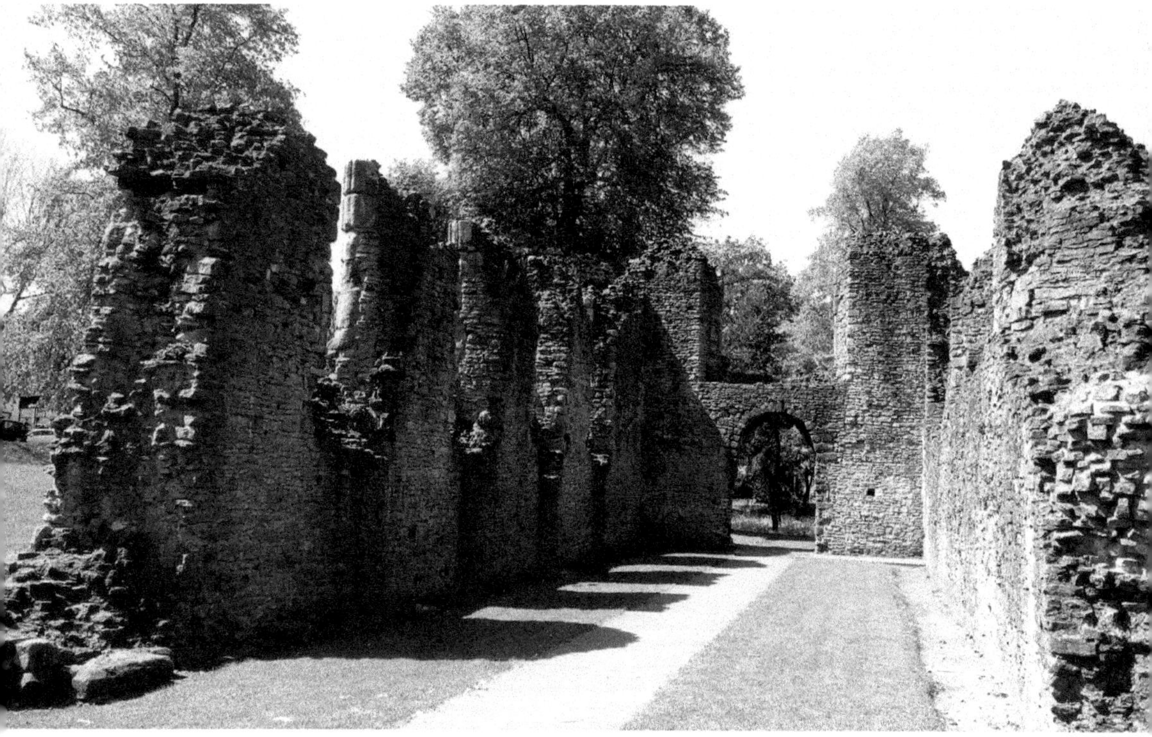

Dudley Priory.

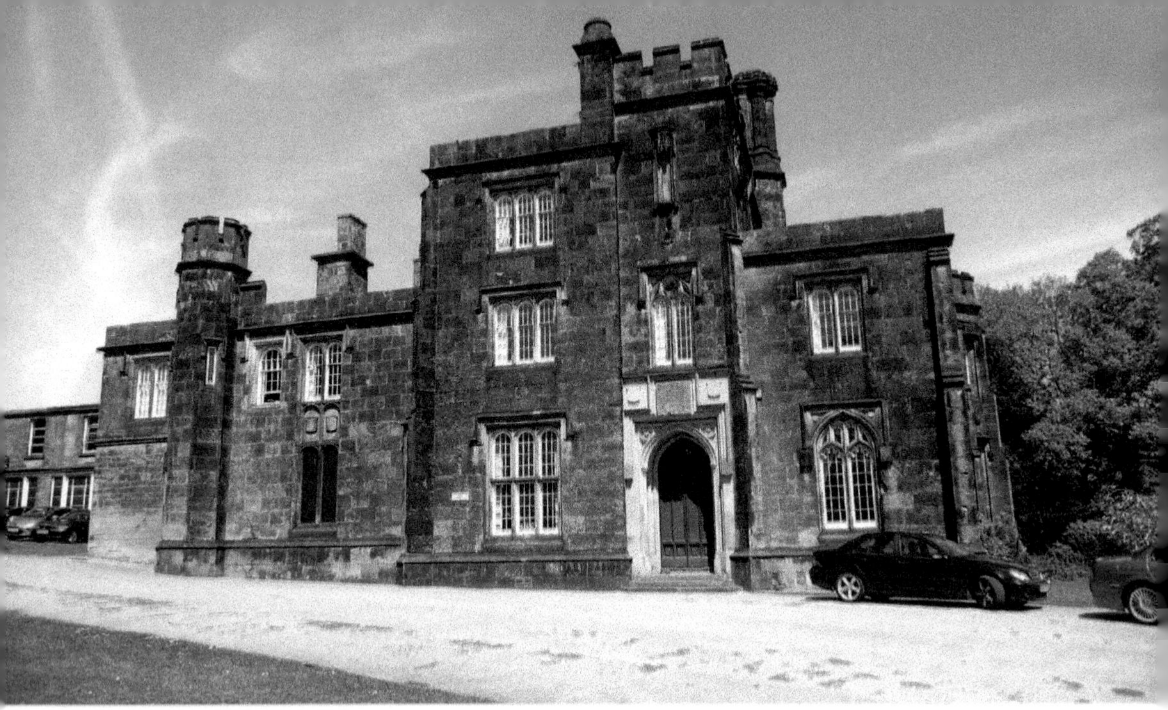

Priory Hall.

5. Stourbridge Glass Quarter

The Stourbridge/Wordsley area has been home to glassmaking for over 400 years, starting as a small cottage-based industry by glassmakers from Lorraine in north-east France in the early 1600s. They were attracted to the area by the existence of rich natural resources: coal for fuel and fireclay for furnaces and melting pots. The first products were glass for windows and bottles. Lead glass tableware production began towards the latter part of the seventeenth century. 'Stourbridge Glass' went on to become a world-renowned mark of quality, reaching its zenith in the Victorian era. After the Second World War the industry went into decline, and sadly today there is little left of the industry. However, there are a number of visitor attractions around that are worthy of a visit.

The Red House Glass Cone Museum and Glassworks Experience in Wordsley is claimed to be the last remaining working glassmaking cone. You can take a canal boat ride to the cone from Stourbridge. Built towards the end of the eighteenth century and used until 1936 when Stuart Crystal moved to Vine Street; this is now one of only four complete cones in the UK. The Grade II listed cone is 90 feet (some say 100 feet) tall and is 60 feet in diameter. Basically a large conical brick chimney with a central furnace at its base, the shape aids the achievement of the extremely high temperature needed to make glass: between 1,500 and 2,500 degree Celsius. Men worked in teams in areas around the furnace known as chairs.

The Glasshouse Heritage Centre (previously the Webb Corbett Visitor Centre) at the Ruskin Glass Centre is on the site of the Royal Doulton factory, Wollaston Road, Amblecote, Stourbridge, DY8 4HF. 01384 399419. email: ruskincraftassociation@outlook.com.

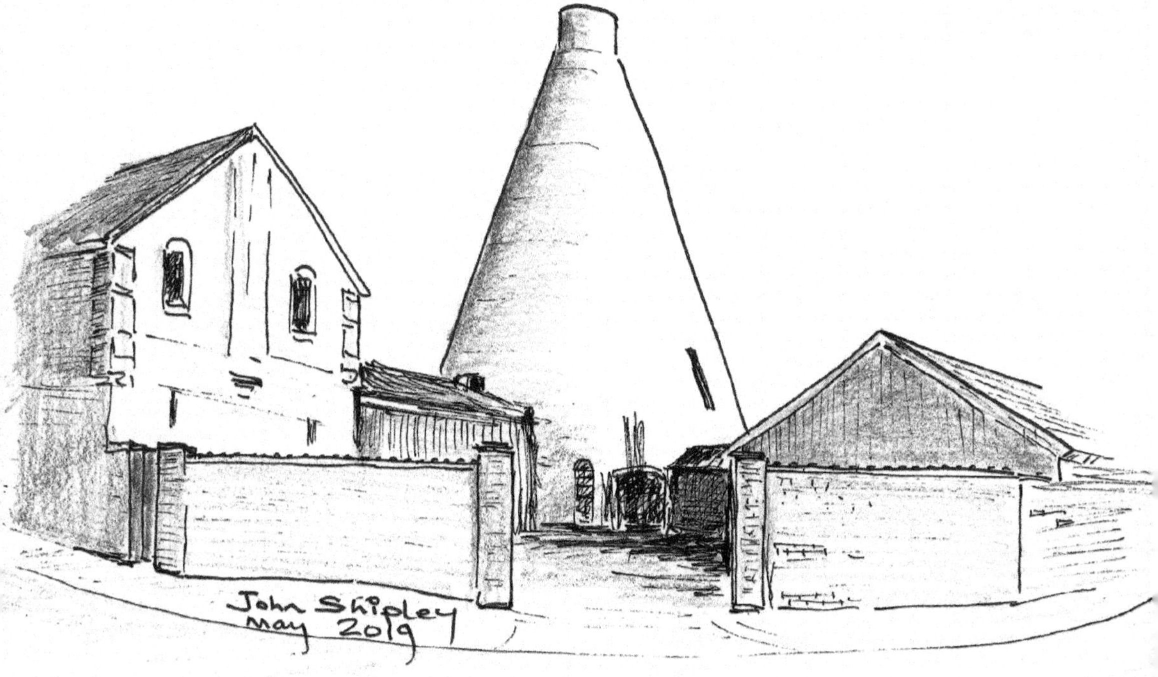

Red House glass cone. (Pen and ink drawing by John Shipley)

Companies with household names, such as Royal Brierley Crystal, Stuart Crystal, Webb Corbett, Royal Doulton and Tudor Crystal, operated in the area, making high-quality products in exquisite full 30 per cent lead crystal. Sadly mass production of hand-cut crystal ended some time ago.

The White House Cone Museum is a new experience scheduled to open in 2020.

There's a Stourbridge Canal and Glass Quarter Heritage Trail to explore and enjoy, and boat trips from the Bonded Warehouse. Check out www.canalboattripsstourbridge.co.uk.

6. Halesowen Abbey

Founded in 1215 by the Order of Canons Regular of Prémontré (White Canons), on land granted by King John, the remains of Halesowen Abbey are to be found at Manor Farm, but can be visited at weekends during the summer. Prémontré is near Laon. The order, formed originally in 1120, were not monks but were canons regular, and followed the Rule of Saint Augustine, a preaching and pastoral ministry. The monastic church was built using local red sandstone. Various sections of the Grade I listed abbey ruins are still visible. Not far from the abbey church is a two-storey building, possibly the abbot's lodgings, dating from around the thirteenth century. Halesowen Abbey was used by pilgrims as a resting place during their pilgrimage. The north barn of Manor Farm, possibly dating from the seventeenth century, was constructed using timber and masonry from the original abbey buildings.

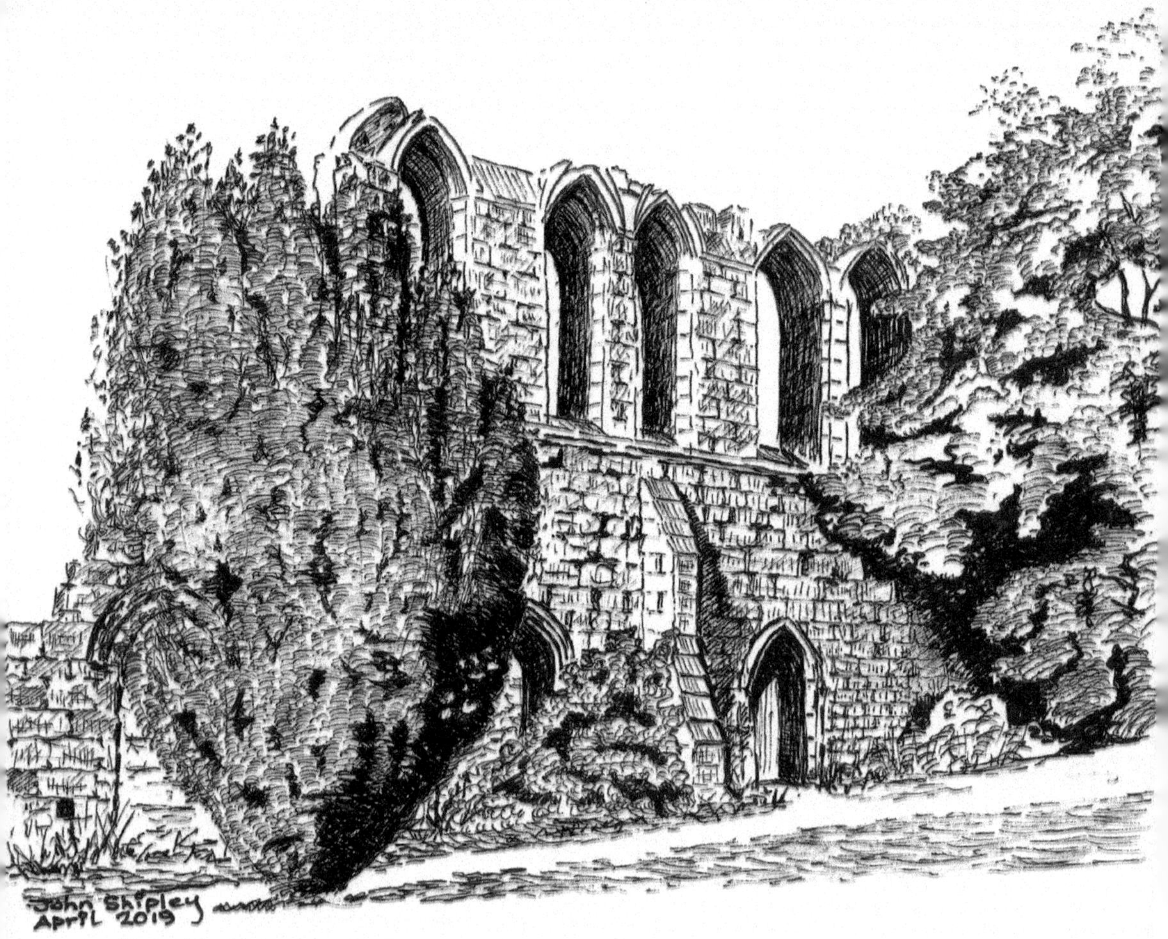

Halesowen Abbey ruins. (Pen and ink drawing by John Shipley)

Following Henry VIII's Dissolution of the Monasteries the king granted the abbey estates to Sir John Dudley, who apparently gave it to his servant.

Location: B62 8RJ. Down a narrow lane off the A456, Manor Way, Halesowen. Check out the English Heritage website for more information.

Standing in the grounds of the Church of St John the Baptist in Halesowen is a medieval cross dating from around 1540, thought to have originated at the abbey. A church, probably of timber construction, was founded here by Roger de Montgomery, 1st Earl of Shrewsbury, on the site of an earlier Saxon church. The cross, once used as a market cross, previously stood in Great Cornbow in the centre of Halesowen, where in 1908 it was blown over in a gale.

Halesowen was once a detached part of Shropshire and has a connection with Warley from the time of the Norman Conquest when sometime after 1066 much of the area was granted to Roger de Montgomery, 1st Earl of Shrewsbury. Halesowen and Warley were then administered from Shropshire as a detached part of that county for the next 600 years – known then as Warley Salop.

The manor of Halas or Hales passed to Dafyd ap Owen, Prince of Wales, in 1177. The two names were combined to make Hales-Owen. The manor later reverting to the Crown, Warley being part of the Manor of Hales-Owen. In 1214 King John bequeathed the manor to the Bishop of Winchester for a religious house to be built by the White Canons. The other part of the area was granted to William FitzAnsculf of Dudley Castle, an area known as Warley Wigorn.

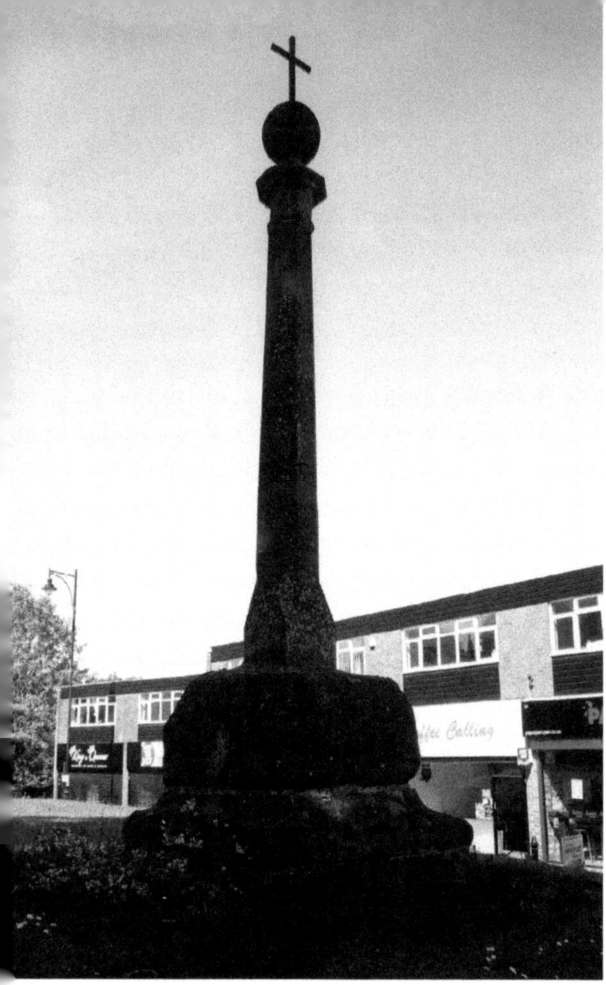

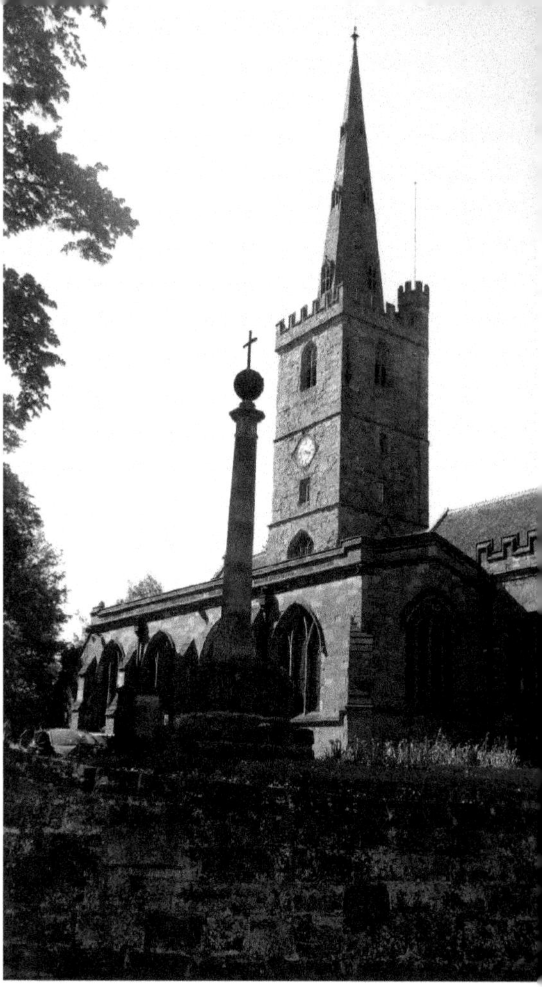

Above left: Medieval cross, Halesowen.

Above right: St John the Baptist Church, Halesowen.

7. Holbeche House, Kingswinford, Hagley Hall, Near Stourbridge, and the Gunpowder Plot

> Remember, remember, the fifth of November, Gunpowder treason and plot
> I see no reason why Gunpowder treason should ever be forgot.

Those of us of a certain age will remember this children's rhyme. However, there are many people who do not know that the failed plot to blow up the James I and his Parliament reached its end near Kingswinford – at Holbeche House to be exact. Holbeche House, built around 1600, was owned by Stephen Lyttelton (Littelton).

It is now a nursing home, and musket ball holes can still be seen in some walls of the Grade II listed building.

The Gunpowder Plot, also known as the Gunpowder Treason Plot and the Jesuit Treason, was cooked up in 1605 by a group of dissident Catholics who planned to rid the country of James I and his lordly government by blowing up the House of Lords during the state opening of Parliament, namely Westminster Hall.

The main plotters were Robert Catesby (said to be the leader), Thomas Percy, brothers John (Jack) and Christopher (Kit) Wright, Guy (Guido) Fawkes, Ambrose Rokewood (Rookwood), Francis Tresham, brothers Thomas and Robert Wintour (Winter), Sir Everard Digby, Robert Keyes, John Grant, and Thomas Bates (Catesby's servant). Other peripheral figures included Stephen Lyttleton of Holbeche, and his uncle, Humphrey Lyttleton of Hagley Park, together with a number of Jesuit priests including Fr Henry Garnet and Fr Edward Oldcorne. Others believed to have engaged in the plot include Henry Morgan, Sir Edward Baynham, Hugh Owen and John Wintour.

As we all know, the plot failed when Guy Fawkes was discovered in the undercroft of Westminster Hall along with thirty-six barrels of gunpowder. The majority of the plotters legged it, stealing supplies from Warwick Castle on 6 November, and weapons and gunpowder from Hewell Grange on the 7th. Sadly while fording the River Stour at Amblecote the powder became damp and unusable, so upon reaching Holbeche House the gunpowder was set out in front of the fire to dry, and – you've guessed it – some time around 10 p.m., a spark leapt from the fire causing the powder to explode, wounding several including Robert Catesby, Ambrose Rokewood and Henry Morgan, and blinding John Grant.

Prior to the explosion Stephen Lyttelton and Thomas Wintour had been sent to seek aid from Sir John Talbot (Robert Wintour's father-in-law, who had refused to go) at his home, nearby Pepperhill at Boningale, but Talbot refused. Lyttelton was all for making a run for it, but Wintour insisted on returning to Holbeche, although once he saw the result of the explosion he too decided to get away. He met up with Lyttelton and the pair made for the Rowley Hills where they were given shelter by farmers Thomas Smart and John Holyhead, and later by John Perkes. The pair, dishevelled and half-starved after many weeks on the run, made their way to Hagley Hall, owned by Meriel Lyttelton (see Hagley Hall), but occupied by Humphrey Lyttelton.

Meanwhile back at Holbeche, Richard Walsh, Sheriff of Worcestershire, and his posse of around 200 men had tracked the powder thieves to the house (they were actually searching for the men who had stolen from Warwick Castle). Surrounding the house they demanded the fugitive's surrender – then the shooting started. Robert Catesby and Thomas Percy were shot and killed in the courtyard at Holbeche, allegedly by the same bullet, along with brothers John (Jack) and Christopher (Kit) Wright. Thomas Wintour, Ambrose Rokewood and John Grant were captured. Sir Everard Digby, Robert Keyes and Thomas Bates were captured later, as were Robert Wintour, Stephen Lyttleton and Humphrey Lyttleton.

At their trial on 27 January 1606, the two Wintour brothers, Digby, Fawkes, Rokewood, Keyes and Bates were found guilty and condemned to be hanged, drawn and quartered. Guy Fawkes foiled his executioners by leaping from the ladder leading to the scaffold, breaking his neck and dying. Francis Tresham died in the Tower of London of a 'natural illness'. Those who had offered aid or refuge were later discovered and dealt with unsympathetically. Stephen Lyttleton was executed at Stafford. Humphrey Lyttelton, John Wintour, Hagley tenant farmer, John Perkes, and his servant, Thomas Burford, were executed at Red Hill near Worcester on 7 April 1606, along with Fr Edward Oldcorne and Fr Ralph Astley. The Earl of Northumberland was imprisoned in the Tower of London until 1621. Fr Nicholas Owen died under torture. Jesuit priest Henry Garnet was executed on 3 May 1606.

The dead bodies of Catesby and Percy were dug up and decapitated, their heads displayed on spikes outside the House of Lords.

Hagley Hall is another West Midlands site associated with the Gunpowder Plot. The present Grade I listed neo-Palladian house was built by George Lyttelton, 1st Lord Lyttleton, replacing an earlier timber-framed structure. Typical of the style of the day the hall has four square corner towers each with a pyramidal roof. Another feature are the Venetian windows.

Hagley Hall's connection with the Gunpowder Plot occurs over fifty years before the construction of the present house. As described previously, following the discovery of the plot the principle plotters made their way to Holbeche House, owned by Stephen Lyttleton, a nephew of Humphrey Lyttleton who resided at Hagley Hall (there is some conjecture about the relationship of the two men some; say uncle and nephew others say brothers). The hall was owned by Meriel Lyttelton, widow of John Lyttelton, who died in the Tower of London in 1601, imprisoned for his part in the Essex rebellion. At that time Meriel was away in London and Humphrey had use of the house. After eight weeks on the run, Stephen Lyttleton and Robert Wintour arrived at Hagley Hall, where Humphrey gave them shelter. Humphrey Lyttelton's cook, John Fynwood, apparently became alarmed at the amount of food his employer was suddenly consuming, and when he spied the two wanted men, he decided to do his duty and inform the authorities, for which he received a pension. Soldiers were dispatched to investigate. Humphrey Lyttleton was adamant that he was harbouring no one; however, a search was carried out. David Bate, another

Holbeche House, near Kingswinford.

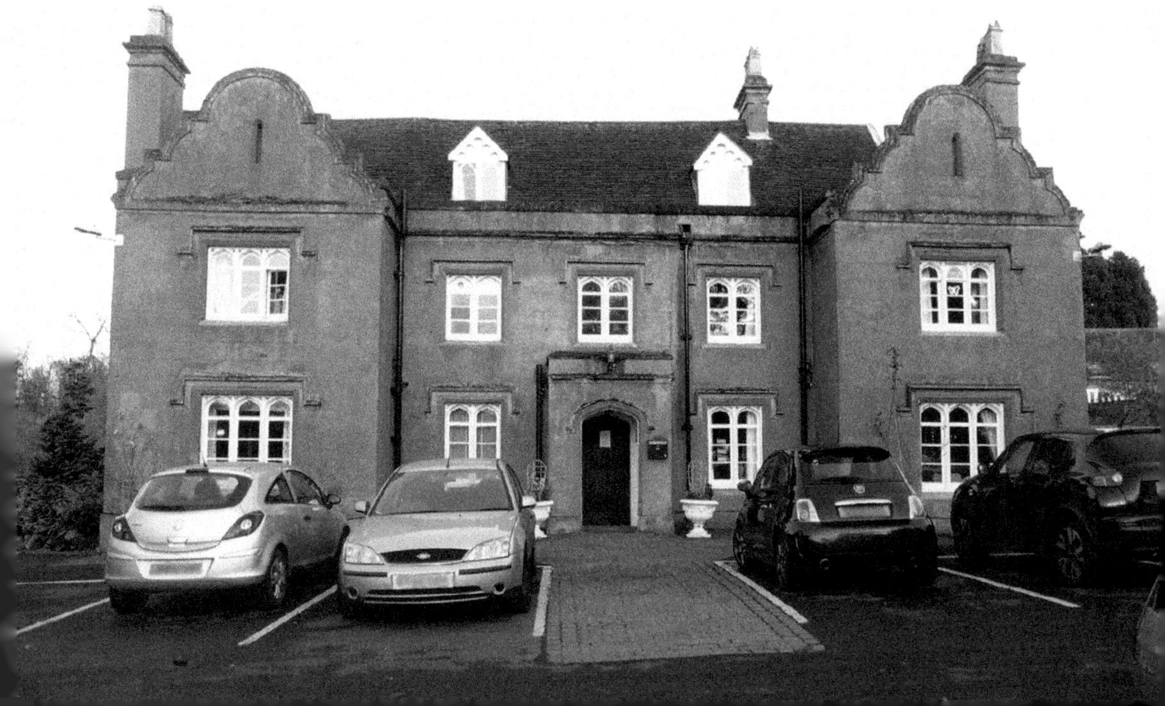

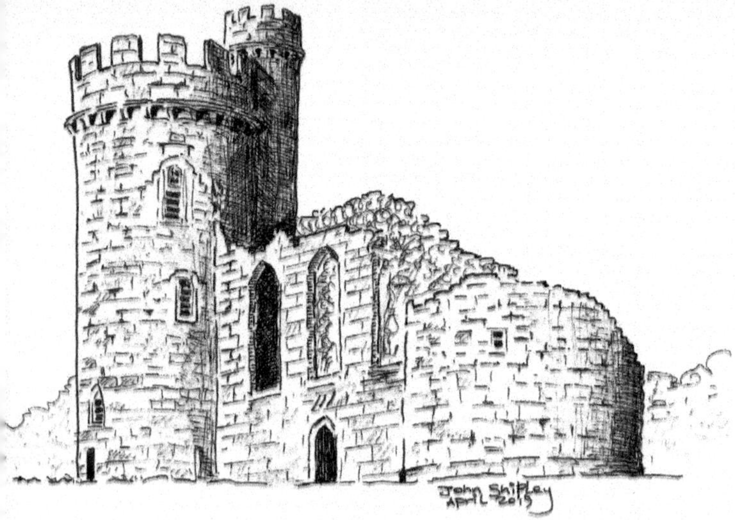

Grade II listed Gothic folly castle, Hagley Hall Park. (Pen and ink drawing by John Shipley.)

servant, showed the soldiers to the courtyard where the two outlaws were seen escaping. The two plotters were arrested on 9 January 1606. Humphrey Lyttleton protested his innocence regarding the plot and managed to escape. He was captured later at Prestwood, but despite his continual protestations he was tried at Worcester and executed at Red Hill, Worcester, on 7 April 1606 along with at least four others.

Guided tours of Hagley Hall are available. Check the website for details: www.hagleyhall.com Address: Hall Drive, Stourbridge, DY5 9LG. Tel: 01562 887290. Parking is free. There is a tearoom, but no picnic areas.

8. Saltwells Nature Reserve

Saltwells Nature Reserve, 247 acres (100 ha), was created in 1981, which includes Saltwells Wood and Netherton Hill (called Knowle Hill from medieval times from the Anglo-Saxon word 'cnol'). The reserve includes two Sites of Special Interest: Doulton's Claypit with its spectacular cliff views and Brewin's Canal Cutting on the Dudley No. 2 canal, a cutting that dates from 1858. The part of Saltwells Wood where evidence of medieval coal mining has been discovered, is classed as a Scheduled Ancient Monument. Coal mining was recorded here from the fourteenth century until the second half of the twentieth century. Netherton Hall once stood on the site just off Cinderbank Road. The hall fell down in 1860 due to mining subsidence. The intriguingly named Tipsyford Brook and Mousesweet Brook run through the reserve, as does the Black Brook, and at Daphne Pool you may catch sight of sixteen species of dragonfly. The name Saltwells comes from the saline waters that sprang from the ground in the area. There was once a brine spa near the Saltwells Inn, where in the eighteenth and early nineteenth centuries people used to bathe and take the waters. In the nineteenth century Saltwells Colliery sank thirty-three pits in the area, many of which suffered from salt water welling up in the mine workings. Hiding in the trees are examples of Jurassic Art sculptures of animals and insects.

Address: Saltwells Lane, Dudley, DY5 1AX.

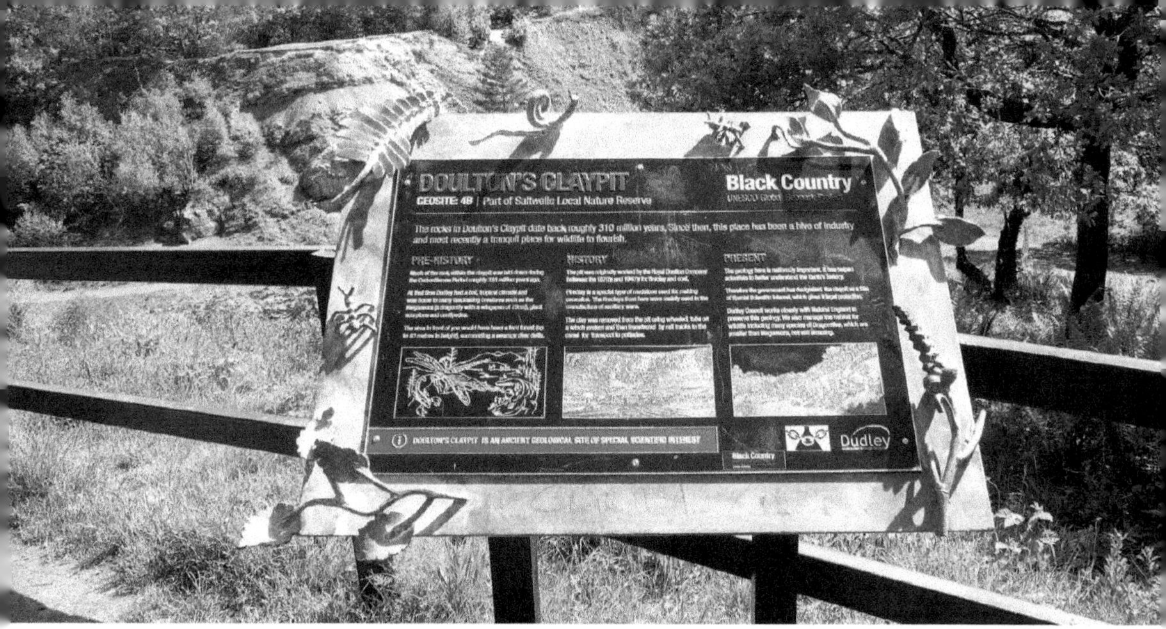

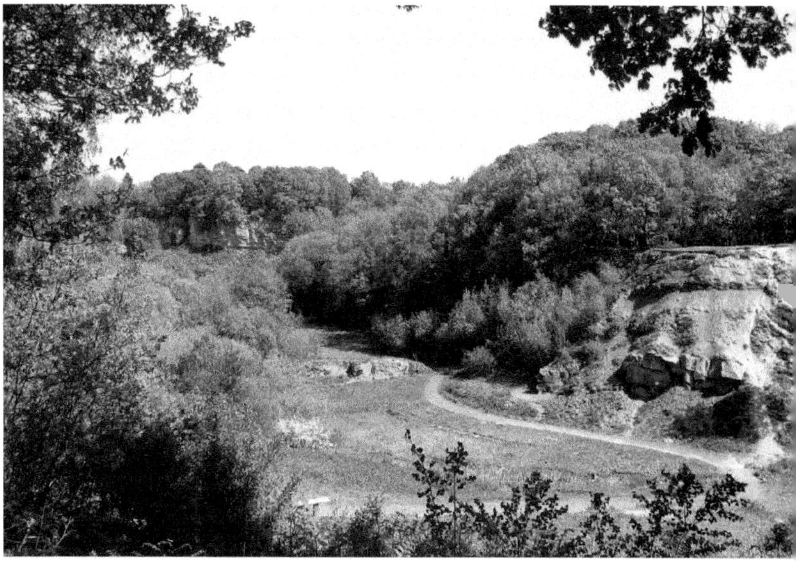

Above: Doulton's Claypit, Saltwells.

Right: Doulton's Claypit, Saltwells.

9. Mushroom Green

The delightfully named Mushroom Green in Netherton is a real gem of the industrial age. The Mushroom Green Chain Shop is open from 2.30 to 5 p.m. on the second Sunday of the month between April and October by Industrial Heritage Stronghold. Admission is free. There are demonstrations of traditional chain making, which began in the area during the eighteenth century, originally on common land on Pensnett Chase. The Enclosure Acts in the eighteenth century saw the land awarded to Viscount Dudley and Ward meaning that the people living there now had to pay rent.

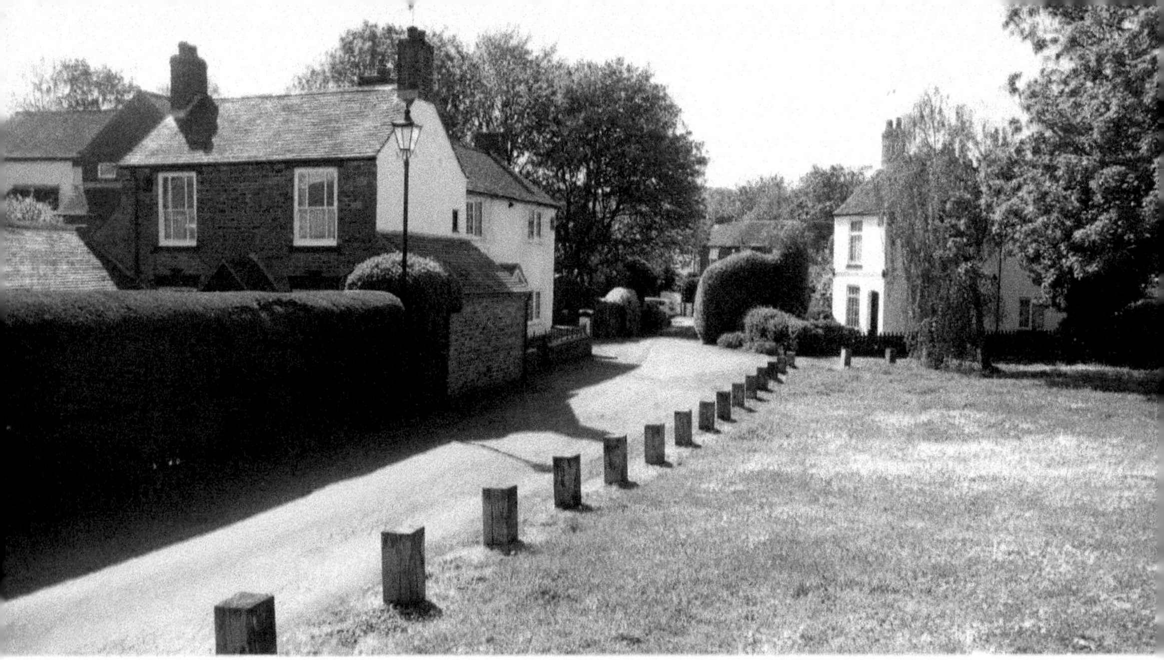

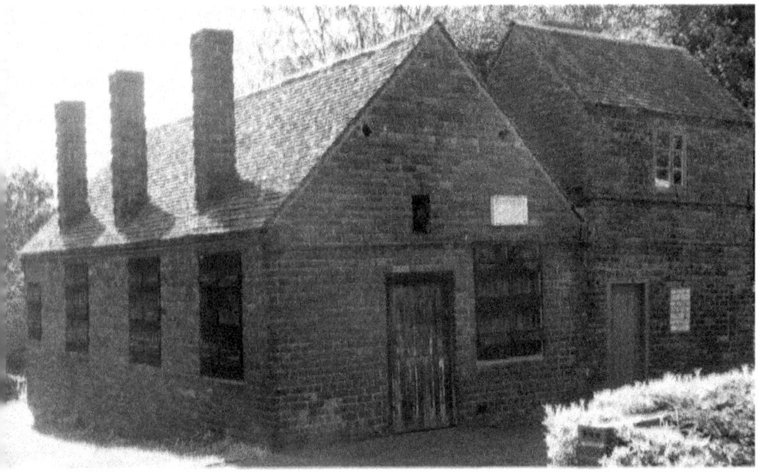

Above: Mushroom Green.

Left: Mushroom Green chain shop.

From the eighteenth century this part of the Black Country was at the heart of chain and nail making, particularly around Netherton, Old Hill and Cradley Heath, where raw materials and skilled workers were in abundance. However, the increasing development of mechanised production techniques saw the decline of these backyard/cottage industries, in which men, women and children were employed. Some did survive into the twentieth century, but only the chain shop at Mushroom Green exists today. This building was restored in the 1970s by the local authority and the Black Country Society.

In 1911, records tell us that 6,550 people were still engaged in chain making, and by the start of the First World War in 1914 the Black Country had earned an international reputation for excellent craftsmanship and top-quality products.

In Cradley Heath there is a 3-metre tall cast steel monument to Lady Chainmakers and the great strike of 1910, depicting a female chain maker with a baby in her arms.

Mushroom Green Chain Shop is located on Quarry Road, Cradley Heath, DY2 0EE.

10. The Crooked House – The Glynne Arms

When I was a kid, my dad took me to this pub on our bikes – lemonade and Smith's crisps for me (remember the little blue packet of salt?). I have visited the place many times subsequently, never ceasing to marvel at how a coin can roll uphill! And on the 'magic table' where a marble can roll uphill! It's not hard to feel a bit drunk as you step inside before having one drink. I reckon it's a 'bostin' plerse'.

Originally built as a farmhouse in 1765, the left side of the building suffered from mining subsidence during the early 1800s when coal mining inadvertently passed under one side, resulting over time in the left side dropping around 4 feet (1.2 metres), but amazingly still intact structurally. Around 1830 it became a public house, taking the name Siden House ('Siden' or 'Sidin' in Black Country spake means 'side-in' or 'crooked') and later the Glynne Arms. In those days the land was owned by Sir Stephen Richard Glynne, 9th Baronet of Bisseter in Oxfordshire. He owned Hawarden Castle in Cheshire, and was the brother-in-law of Liberal Prime Minister William Gladstone. Glynne was also part owner of the Oak Farm Iron and Brick Works Company, Kingwinford. With his business failing when he died on 17 June 1874, the building was sold.

In the 1940s the building was condemned as being unsafe and was scheduled for demolition until Wolverhampton and Dudley Breweries (known in the Black Country as Bonks's) stepped in, bought the pub and had the building stabilised with brick buttresses and steel girders, and thankfully left the building canted around 15 degrees. It's a great place for a pint, but watch out for the wonky and droopy nature of the walls and doors.

The Crooked House.

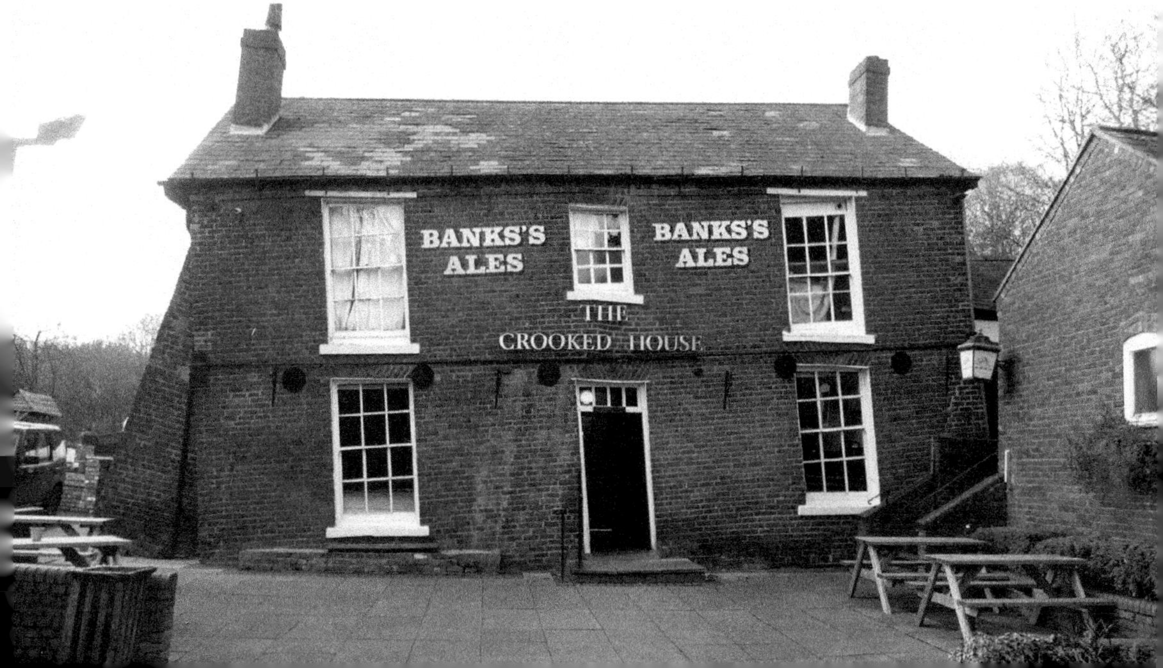

The Crooked House can be found just off the B4176 Himley Road, down the winding Crooked House Lane, under a couple of bridges; keep going and you will eventually reach the pub. On the way you will encounter a few crazy signs such as 'Beware The Bend Or Yow'll End Up In The Cut'.

Website: www.thecrooked-house.co.uk. Telephone: 01384 238583.

11. Barrow Hill Nature Reserve and Pensnett Volcano

At the heart of Barrow Hill Nature Reserve in Pensnett is an extinct volcano known as the Dudley Volcano. The dome-shaped hill consists of dolerite (basalt), a hard rock formed from the magma that once spewed from the volcano during the Carboniferous Period over 300 million years ago. In those long-off days prior to the Continental Drift when the earth's tectonic plates moved to their present locations, the entire area around Dudley, part of the Pennine Basin, was near the equator with much of it underwater. Surges of ash and agglomerates in this period helped the formation of Etruria Marl, and from its clays the local brick-making industry grew. Dolerite was mined for road surfaces.

Barrow Hill rises to 500 feet (152 metres) above sea level and gets its name from the discovery of two Bronze Age barrows (burial chambers) on its northern slopes believed to date from between 2000 BC and 700 BC, although sadly quarrying has destroyed all traces of the barrows. A large cross denotes the summit of the hill.

Declared a Local Nature Reserve in July 2005 with the aim of preserving the area's geology and wildlife habitats, the ancient woodlands of ash, beech and sycamore are just a tiny fragment of what was once Pensnett Chase, which coverd a vast area that in the thirteenth century and was hunted by Baron Dudley of Dudley Castle and his retinue.

Today visitors can walk through Speckled Wood, around Coopers Bank Farm with its haybarn and meadows, see Hunt's Mill Farm (the mill built prior to 1780 was demolished in 1986), and the Old Colliery Pump House Chimney.

The name Pensnett is derived from 'Pen', the Celtic word for a 'hillside', and Sneath, Anglo-Saxon for a 'small fenced area'.

Until the mid-nineteenth century the area was a hive of charcoal burning, set amid the ironworks, quarries and coal mines that developed in the seventeenth and eighteenth centuries. This is reputedly where in 1665 Dud Dudley, illegitimate son of Lord Dudley, first smelted iron ore using coal instead of charcoal, although it wasn't until 1709 when Wren's Nest-born Abraham Darby (he was descended from Dud Dudley's sister Jane) perfected the technique in Coalbrookdale that the Industrial Revolution really began.

An informative leaflet is available about the area. The reserve is to be found at Vicarage Lane, Pensnett, DY5 4JH. There is limited parking near St Mark's Church, Pensnett, plus a small car park off Merryfield Road, Dudley, DY1 2NS.

12. The Fountain Inn and the Tipton Slasher

'Now 'ere's a fermus bloke o' the Black Country – 'is nicknerm wuz "THE TIPTON SLASHER", but 'is real nerm wuz William Perry, and 'ee wuz born in Tipton in 1819. And 'is name is featured on the sign at the Fountain Inn in Tipton, because that's where he made his headquarters'.

Bare-knuckle boxer William Perry was the third of five children. His parents were Timothy, a miner, and Sarah Perry. Despite having the disadvantage of a 'K leg' (knock-knees) William Perry grew up tough and strong, and by the age of sixteen found himself in London working as a navvy.

His first recorded fist fight was on 3 November 1835 against Barney Dogherty in a bizarre contest. The first seven rounds took place opposite the Ship Inn, Mortlake, paused when police interrupted proceedings, then restarted on Lechmere Common where after another seven rounds Perry emerged victorious. His second recorded bout was against Birmingham pugilist Ben Spilsbury on 27 December 1836. The contest took place in Oldbury, which Perry won after nineteen bloody rounds, severely cutting or slashing the face of his opponent. Legend has it that it was after this fight that Perry was given the nickname 'The Tipton Slasher'. Next up was Jem Scunner from Gornal, who Perry fought on 22 November 1837. The fight was reportedly staged over two days for £25 a side. The early rounds took place near Gornal, resuming the following day at Kingswood, near Codsall. After a staggering thirty-one rounds Perry was declared the winner.

Perry's prowess as a pugilist caught the attention of boxer Johnny Broome, who astutely decided he would promote Perry's future fights, setting the next fight against James 'Deaf' Burke. However, the fight, scheduled for August 1842, was cancelled when Broome failed to put up the deposit of the agreed stake on the due date.

Perry's next opponent was American giant Charles Freeman, an ex-circus performer reckoned to be around 6 feet 10 inches tall and weighing over 18 stones. Perry was just over 6 feet and weighed around 13 stones. Freeman had been brought to England from America in 1842 by Ben (Big Ben) Caunt, another British boxer. After seventy plus rounds, on 14 December 1842, the match was declared a draw when darkness fell on the two protagonists. Six days later the rematch ended bizarrely when, after thirty-eight rounds, Perry fell to the floor without being struck by Freeman, and thus the big American was declared the winner. Following this Perry fought a number of exhibition bouts around the country arranged by Johnny Broome.

Perry's next three fights were all against Tass Parker from West Bromwich, and again were not without incident. The first, on 19 December 1843 on Dartford Marshes, was declared a draw when the police intervened after fifty-seven rounds. In February 1844, Perry and Parker technically fought again. This time Parker went down without being hit and Perry was declared the victor. On 4 August 1846 on Lindrick Common, Perry was the victor in their third fight.

On 17 December 1850 Perry fought Tom Paddock on Woking Common for £100 a-side, Perry winning after twenty-seven gruelling rounds. After winning this fight Perry claimed the Championship of England.

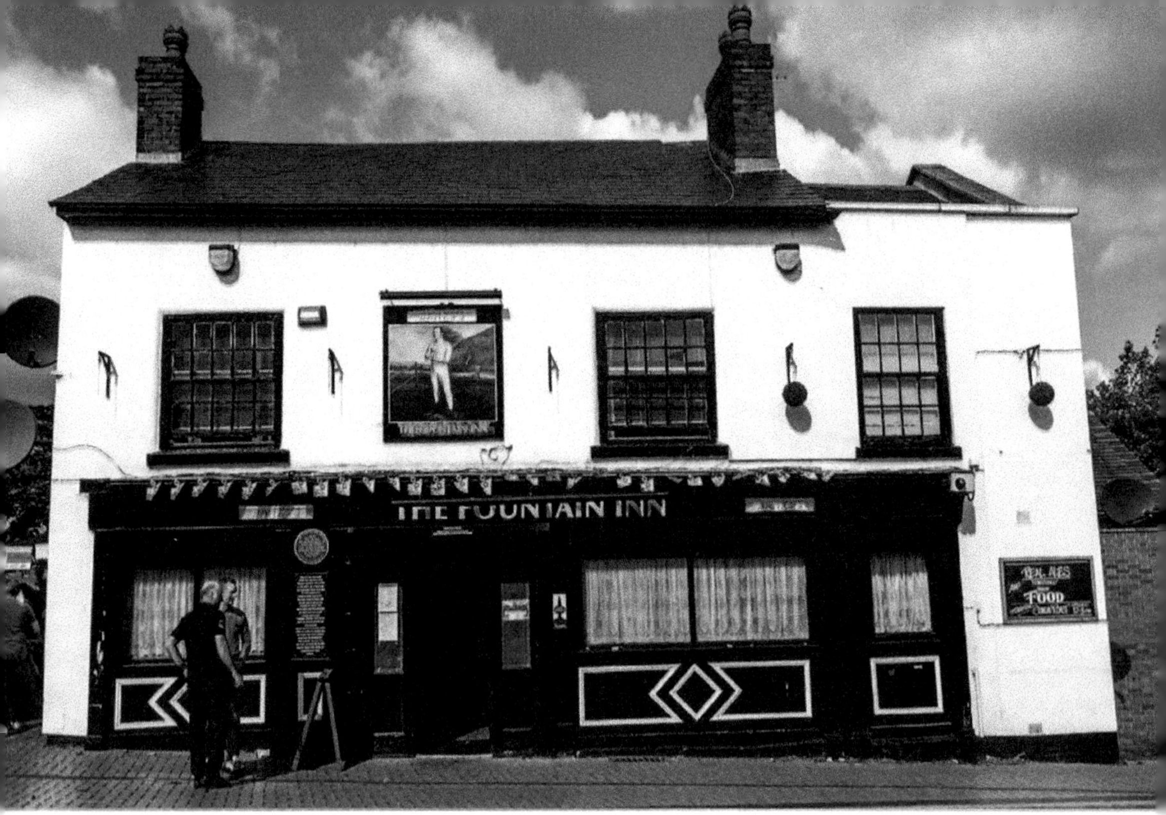

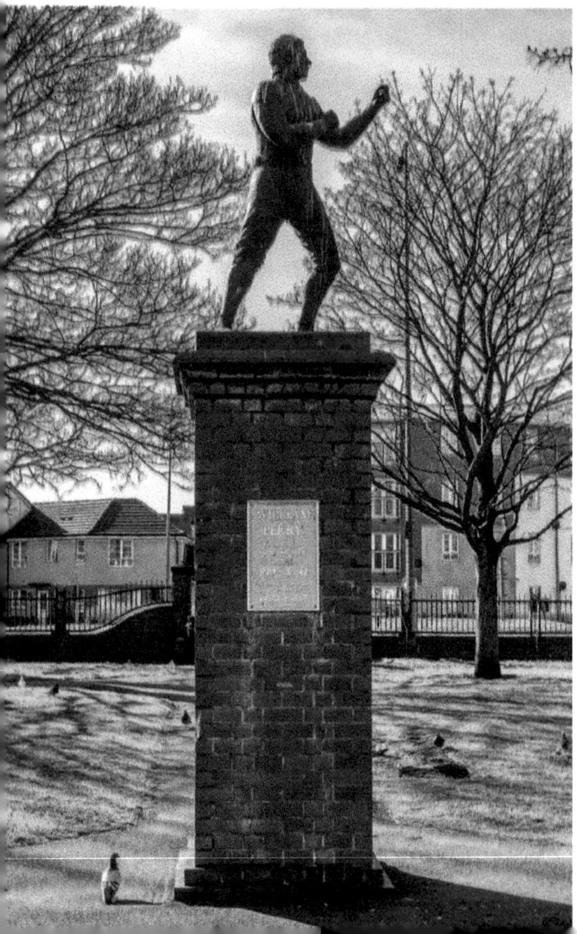

Above: The Fountain Inn, Tipton. (Courtesy of Phil Wild)

Left: Statue of William Perry, the Tipton Slasher, Coronation Gardens, Tipton. (Courtesy of Phil Wild)

William Perry's next match involved matrimony when he married Ann Maria Challingworth on 11 June 1851.

Perry next took on Johnny Broome's brother, Harry Broome, on 29 September 1851, but was disqualified for hitting Broome when his opponent was on his knees. Harry Broome subsequently claimed the Championship of England. The pair signed articles for a rematch at £25 a side, but Harry Broome forfeited the match fee, preferring not to fight the Slasher again. Perry then reclaimed the Champion of England title.

Perry set up a beerhouse in Spon Lane, West Bromwich, which he renamed 'The Champion of England'. it was formerly known as the George, and he was licensee from 1852 to 1857.

William Perry's final recorded fight was against Tom Sayers on 16 June 1857 on the Isle of Grain, Medway, Kent. Despite being a much smaller man – reports put Sayers at around 5 feet 8 inches tall, weighing less than 11 stones – Sayers won the fight after ten rounds. As well as losing this fight the Slasher lost most of his money as he'd sold his pub and bet everything on a victory for himself.

Perry subsequently became the landlord of the Bricklayer's Arms, sometimes known as the Old Bricklayer's Arms and the Bricklayer's Tavern, Walsall Road, Wolverhampton. He took to drink and worked on the canals.

Sadly William Perry died on 24 December 1880 of alcoholism and pulmonary congestion at his Bilston home. He was buried at St John's Church, Kates Hill, Dudley.

A bronze statue of William Perry, by Bill Haynes, unveiled on 3 May 1993, stands proudly in Coronation Gardens in Tipton, not far from the Fountain Inn.

In 1984 the Fountain Inn (No. 51 Owen Street, Tipton, DY4 8HE) was granted Grade II listed building status in recognition of its connection with William Perry, who regularly fought fellow boatmen on the many local canals in order to be first through the lockgates.

The Tipton Slasher and Tom Sayers are mentioned in Robert Browning's poem 'A Likeness'.

13. Cotwall End Local Nature Reserve

Cotwall End Nature Reserve is a vibrant mixture of ancient woodland where coal mining once took place. Established before the reign of Edward III, Cotwall was a tiny hamlet of one or two farms. There are numerous springs across the site. Bob's Brook is the headwater of the River Stour. Sugarwell Pool is fed by sweet-water springs and is part of the Ellowes Hall estate that contained a series of ornamental pools. Ellowes Hall was built using local stone in 1821 by ironmaster John Turton Fereday. Sadly the house was demolished in 1964 following a fire, and a school now occupies the site. Four coal seams were found in the valley including the famous 10-yard-thick Staffordshire coal seam. Other quality natural resources occurring in the valley are clay for high-quality bricks and sandstones used as grinding stones.

A 2-mile circular trail takes in Turner's Hill Wood, a Site of Special Scientific Interest, the Dingle and the Finney.

Address: The Alley, Dudley, DY3 2UL. There's a small car park on Cotwall End Road.

Brockswood Animal Sanctuary (previously Critters Farm) is a 16-acre site at the bottom end of Catholic Lane, where all manner of animals are cared for and rehabilitated. A replica Anglo-Saxon village is being created on the site by 'Age of Penda', a Dark Age re-enactment society based at Brockwood.

Address: Catholic Lane, Dudley, DY3 3YE. Tel: 01902 884390. Website: www.brockswood.org.

14. Wychbury Ring, near Stourbridge

This multivallate Iron Age hill fort, on Wychbury Hill, the westernmost point of the Clent Hills, is around 820 feet (250 metres) east to west, and 490 feet (150 metres) north to south, roughly covering an area of 7.25 acres (2.93 ha). The fort has two fortified in-turned entrances and two sets of ramparts. Bronze rings plus Roman coins have been found nearby. The site is mostly covered in trees.

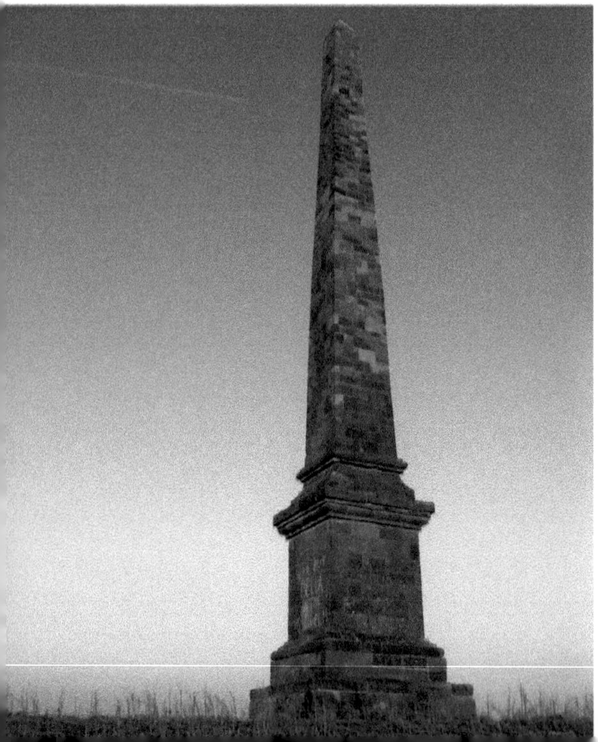

Wychbury Obelisk. (Courtesy of Naomi Holdstock)

Wychbury Hill with its ancient twenty-eight-tree yew grove is the scene of a murder mystery. In 1943 the skeleton of an unknown woman was discovered by four boys in the hollow trunk of a yew tree in nearby Hagley Woods.

In 1944 graffiti first appeared in Birmingham and then on the Wychbury Obelisk: 'Who put Bella in the Wych Elm – Hagley Wood?' Forensic examination placed the time of death on or before October 1941. Who the woman was remains a mystery, although there are some conjectural theories surrounding her identity. The graffiti mysteriously kept reappearing each time it was cleaned off.

The hill is just off the A456 Birmingham Road and from there the Grade II listed Wychbury Obelisk can be seen. Also on the hill on part of the estate owned by the 12th Viscount Cobham, Christopher Charles Lyttelton, is a Greek Doric Temple of Theseus folly, built around 1758, now dilapidated and heavily vandalised; These days it's fenced off and not open to the public.

The name Wychbury is derived from a Saxon sub-kingdom of Mercia belonging to the Hwicce people.

15. Himley Hall and Park

Adjacent to Himley's medieval Church of St Michael and All Angels, directly across the Stourbridge Road from Himley village, once stood Himley Hall, a moated manor house that for over 400 years was one of the homes of the Lords of Dudley, along with Dudley Castle.

In 1645, during the early days of the First English Civil War, Charles I and his retinue, en route to fight the Battle of Naseby (which of course Charles lost), used the grounds of Himley Hall for their main encampment.

Himley Hall.

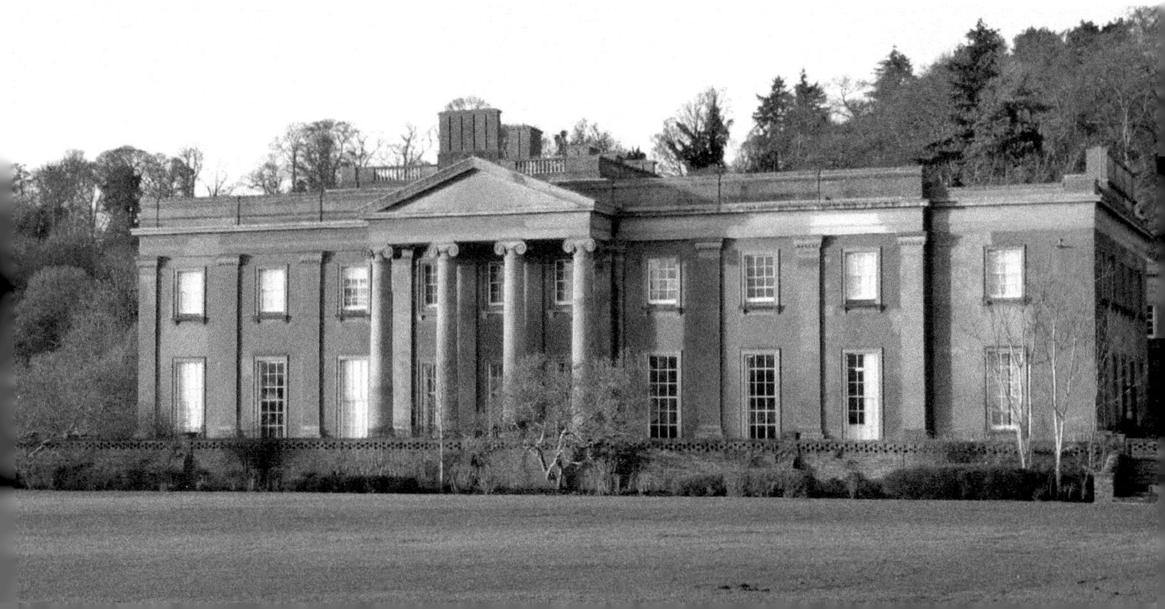

In 1643 the Barony of Dudley passed to Humble (yes that was his Christian name) Ward when in 1628 he married Frances Sutton, 6th Baroness Dudley and sole heiress to the Dudley estates. Humble's father, William Ward, was a wealthy London goldsmith and jeweller to the court of Charles I, who had purchased the debts of the 5th Lord Dudley (Frances' grandfather). Following the slighting of Dudley Castle during the English Civil War, the family regarded Himley Hall as their principal residence. In the seventeenth century industrial pioneer Dud (Dudd) Dudley once lived at the hall.

Born in 1598, Dud Dudley was the illegitimate son of Edward Sutton, 5th Baron Dudley. Dud began experimenting with alternative methods of smelting iron ore with coal at his father's works at Pensnett Chase and the legendary Cradley Forge, probably the earliest significant metal working on the River Stour. His groundbreaking book *Mettallum Martis*, published in 1665, pioneered the methods that defined the way metal was smelted. Abraham Darby is descended from Dud Dudley's sister Jane. Dud died in 1684, at the age of eighty-five.

In 1740, John Ward, 6th Lord Ward, inherited the estate and decided he needed a more impressive home, so he had the old manor house demolished and built a new Himley Hall further from the road. This classical Palladian-style mansion was quickly extended and additional wings were added. In 1764, he had Himley village moved and the church re-erected on its present site. John's son, also John, employed Lancelot 'Capability' Brown to redesign the parkland, including a great lake plus a new carriage approach to the hall from the Dudley Road. In all around 180 acres of parkland were remodelled during the 1770s.

In 1860, the title Earl of Dudley was recreated and bestowed on the 11th Lord Ward. Prior to this the earl had purchased Witley Court in Worcestershire to be the family's principal residence. Himley Hall now became home to the Dowager Lady Ward, Lord Ward's mother, and his sister, the Hon. Rachel Ward. In 1920, Witley Court was sold and Himley Hall became the family home once again. Members of the royal family were frequent visitors.

During the Second World War the south wing was used as a Red Cross hospital, and after the conflict the National Coal Board bought the estate for £45,000 to use as their regional headquarters. Around this time fire gutted the south wing, which was rebuilt. In 1966 Dudley and Wolverhampton District Councils jointly bought the estate from the Coal Board, and the park was subsequently opened as a public leisure area. In 1988 Dudley Council became sole owners after buying out Wolverhampton's share, commencing restoration work in 1992. It's now a multi-use centre, with an elegant art deco-style banqueting suite and lounge bar.

Address: Dudley, DY3 4DF. Website: www.himleyhallandpark.co.uk.

16. The Leasowes

Leasowes Park just off Mucklow Hill, Halesowen, is a Grade I listed historic lansdcaped garden park designed by poet William Shenstone and laid out between 1743 and 1763. The 57 acres (around 141 ha) of open grassland, woodland walks, lakes, cascade and streams rank alongside those at Blenheim Palace and Stowe. On 5 November 1714 Thomas and Anne Shenstone (William's parents) moved from nearby Lapal to The Leasowes, a dairy farm. When Shenstone died in 1763 the estate was purchased by Edward Horne, who, in around 1776, pulled down Shenstone's house and built another in its place, together with a walled garden and a hothouse. Various future owners followed, but in the 1820s the park was described as being in a state of ruin and desolation. Fortunately Halesowen Council stepped in to acquire the site, part of which is occupied by the Halesowen Golf Club, formed in 1906. The historic building is now the clubhouse.

The remainder of the park is open to the public. A leaflet is available. Parking is on Leasowes Lane, off Mucklow Hill – A458. The southern end of the park borders Manor Lane A456.

Address: Leasowes Lane, Off Mucklow Hill, Halesowen, B62 8DH.

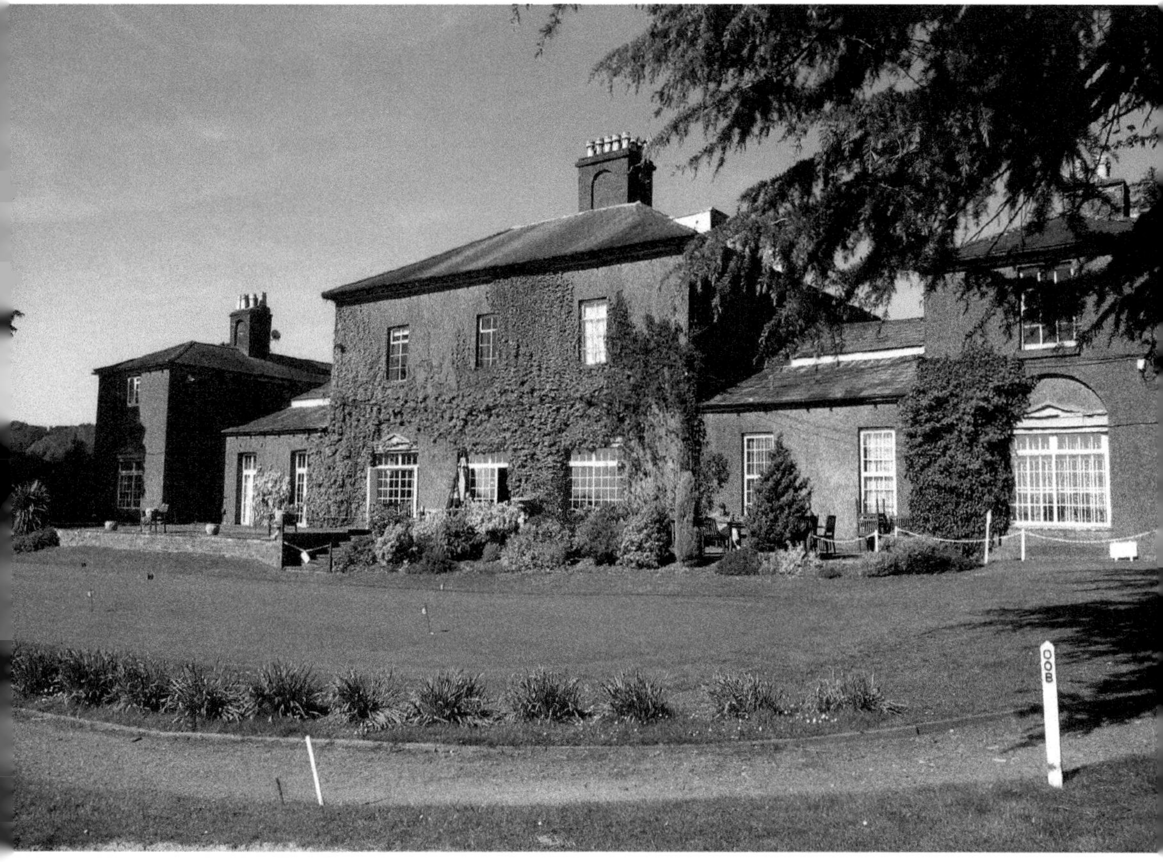

The Leasowes, now the clubhouse of Halesowen Golf Club.

The Sandwell Metropolitan Borough Area

This borough was formed 1 April 1974, comprising of six amalgamated towns that have many sub-districts. It was named after the holy 'Sand Well' located in Sandwell Valley.

17. The Oak House, West Bromwich

The Oak House is a wonderfully atmospheric Elizabethan black-and-white, timber-framed building in the heart of West Bromwich, built around 1630 or possibly earlier, with brick additions in the 1650s. It was home to a yeoman farmer John Turton and his

The Oak House, West Bromwich.

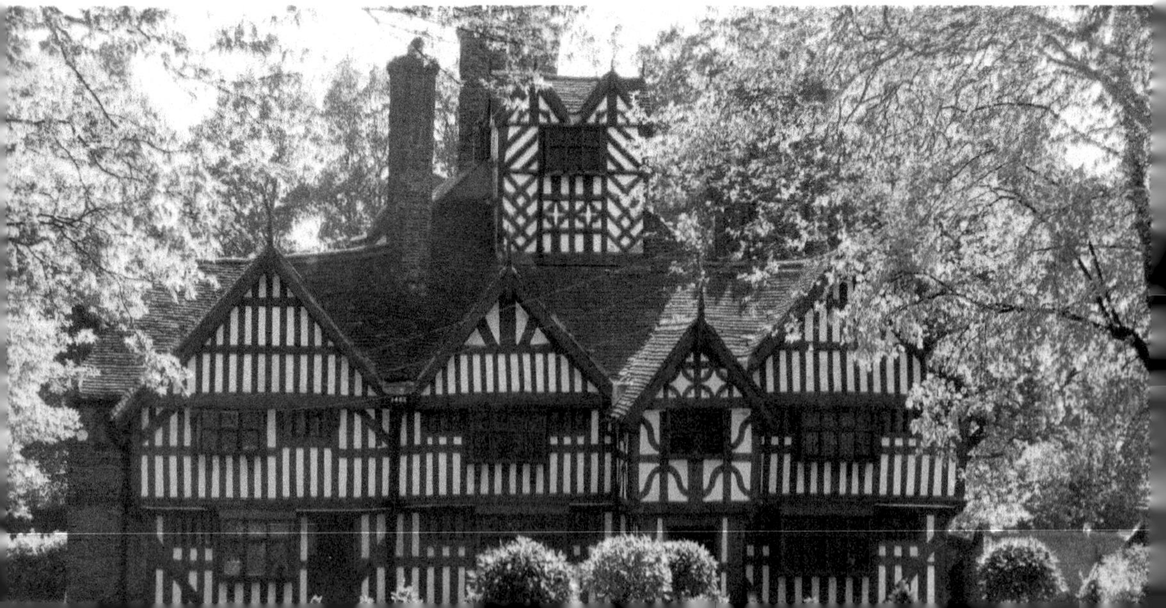

family from at least 1634 until 1788, when the house passed to William Whyley. Apart from farming John Turton was also into nail making and moneylending (known as gulgropers) – making loans to impoverished Royalist gentry after the English Civil War.

The free-to-enter museum boasts examples of fine panelling, and is furnished with period pieces from the seventeenth century. The Oak House is set in its own grounds, which include a children's playground. The historic barns were opened in 2014. There is also a seventeenth-century dairy and servant's bedroom. It is, of course, one of the oldest buildings in the area.

Address: Oak Road, Greets Green, West Bromwich, B70 8HJ.

18. Sandwell Valley Country Park, Sandwell Priory, Priory Woods Local Nature Reserve, Sandwell Park Farm, and Sot's Hole Local Nature Reserve

Sandwell Valley is a true nature reserve, spread over 1,300 acres of countryside, where some time around AD 1190 the Benedictine Sandwell Priory was founded by William de Offini, on the site of an ancient hermitage situated near a holy well known as the 'Sand Well' from which the area takes its name. The well is also known as St Augustine's Well. In earlier times ownership of the site was in the hands of the Sutton and Dudley families. In 1525 the priory was in a ruinous state with only two monks left, and so Edward, Lord Dudley, agreed to Cardinal Wolsey's dissolution of the priory, who wanted to use the money for his own projects. During the English Civil War the priory was owned by Royalist Brome Whorwood, and thus was sequestered by the Parliamentarians. In 1701 William, Baron Dartmouth, created 1st Earl of Dartmouth in 1711, bought the estate as his Staffordshire seat and began sinking coal-mining pits. Between 1703 and 1708 the house was remodelled, parts of which were pulled down and rebuilt in brick, incorporating some of the old structure. The west side was extended in 1840. A few years later the 4th Earl purchased Patshull Hall and relocated there. Sandwell Hall had many subsequent uses before being demolished in 1928 due to mining subsidence caused by Hampstead Colliery. West Bromwich Corporation purchased the land from the 7th Earl in order to preserve the area as open countryside.

Priory Woods Local Nature Reserve is also part of Sandwell Valley Country Park. It has more than 51 acres (21 ha) of mature woodland, pools and grassland. The island on Ice House Pool houses a heronry. Access is via Sandwell Park Farm and Park Lane. Tel: 0121 553 0220.

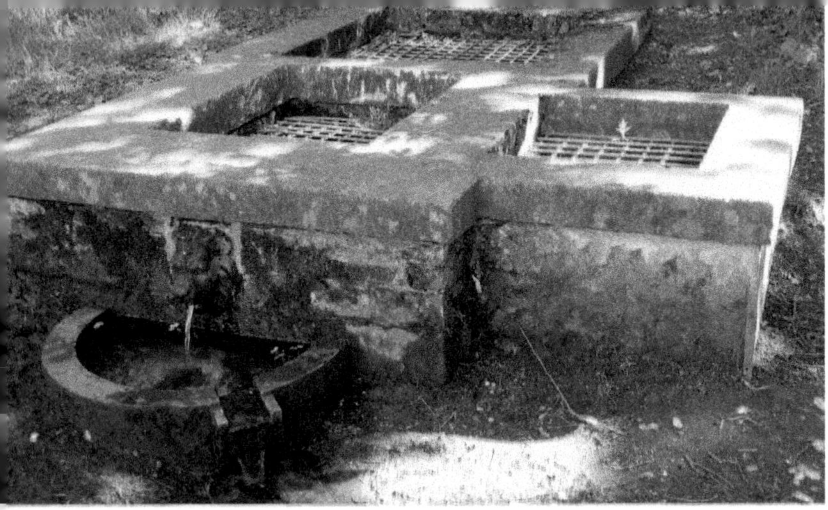

St Augustine's Well (the Sand Well), Sandwell Valley, West Bromwich.

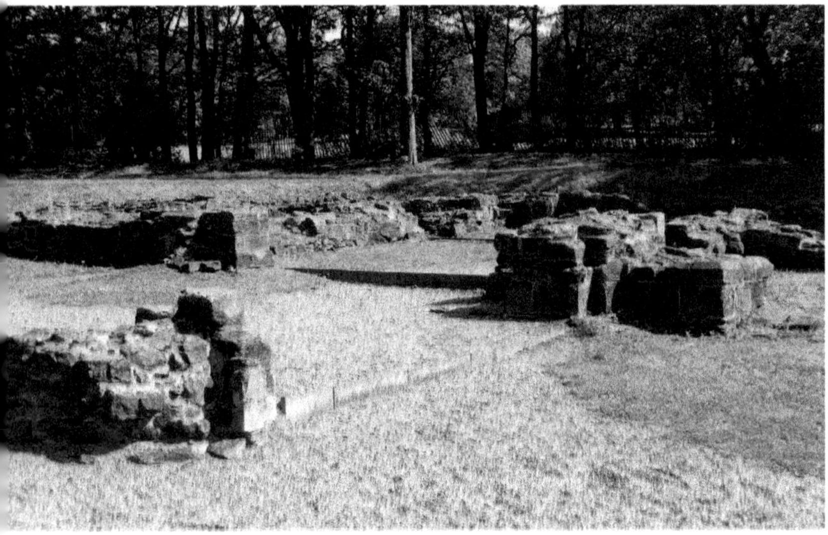

Sandwell Priory ruins.

Standing on a traffic island just outside West Bromwich where the A41 meets Junction 1 of the M5 Motorway is the Grade II listed Sandwell Arch, once a lodge and entrance gateway (the only one to survive) to Sandwell Hall and the Dartmouth estate, and latterly to Sandwell Golf Club. There is a passing resemblance to a triumphal Roman arch, but sadly this is not Roman – it dates from around 1738.

Sandwell Valley Sailing Club house is situated in the old pithead baths building of the Jubilee Colliery that once operated on the site. A tramway once linked the Jubilee to the Sandwell Park Colliery. Excavations on the Jubilee site have revealed the base of the chimney stack and upcast engine house. Website: www.svsc.co.uk.

The Grade II listed Sandwell Park Farm visitor centre is situated a short distance from the site of Sandwell Hall. On this historic restored working farm there are rare breeds of farm animals to see such as Hereford cattle, Shropshire sheep, Tamworth pigs and various rare breeds of poultry. There's also a walled kitchen garden, which is around one-quarter of its nineteenth-century size, a small games area, gift shop and museum, plus an award-winning tearoom.

On the east side of Forge Lane, around where the road changes its name to Park Lane, is the entrance to another section of Sandwell Valley Country Park, bordered by the River Tame. Here you can find Forge Mill Farm, Forge Mill Lake and Sandwell Valley Bird Sanctuary.

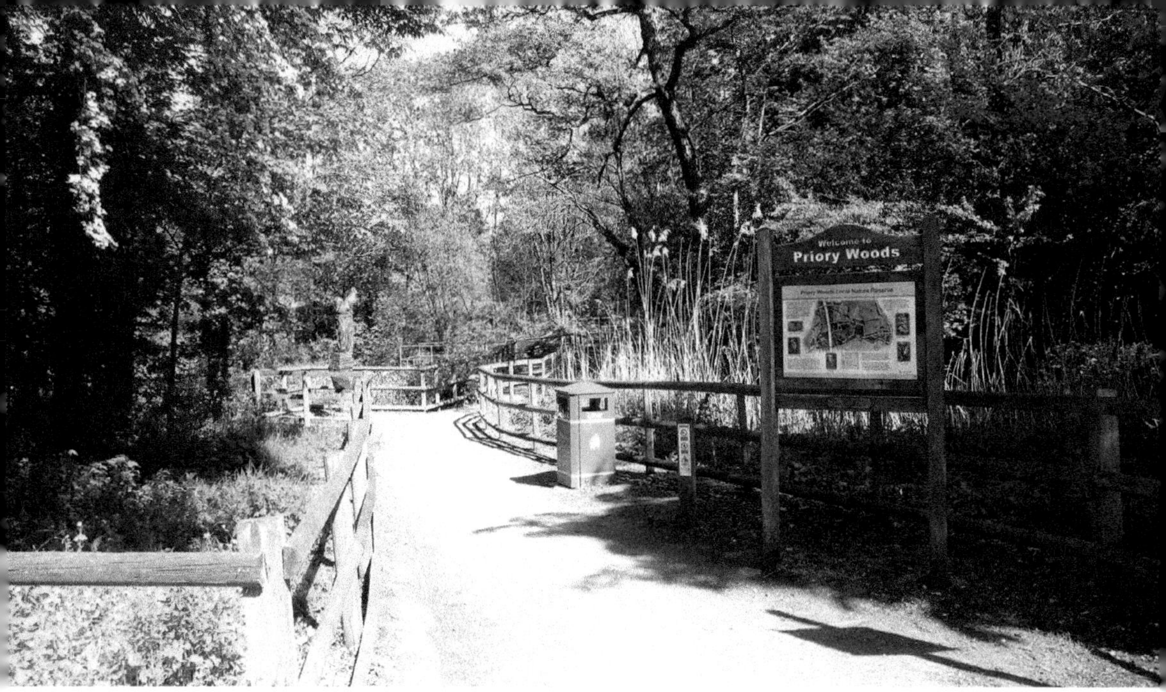

Above: Priory Woods, Sandwell Valley, West Bromwich.

Right: The Sandwell Arch. (Pen and ink drawing by John Shipley)

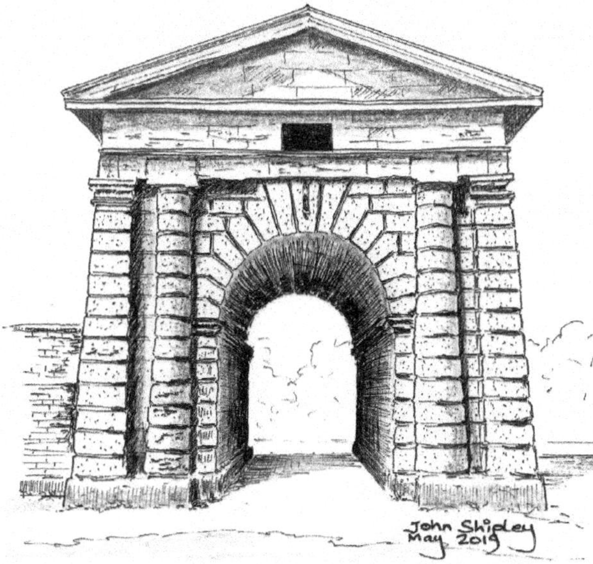

There are car parks on Park Lane, near the Swan Pool and at the access point to Forge Mill Lake. The main entrance to Sandwell Valley Country Park is via Salter's Lane to the car park. Access can also be found through nearby Dartmouth Park. All are pay and display £2 per day currently. Check the website for details: www.sandwell.gov.uk/info/200249/parks_in_sandwell/1023/sandwell_valley_country_park.

Sot's Hole Local Nature Reserve is spread over 13.5 acres (5.5 ha), with some of the oldest (semi-ancient) woodland in the Sandwell area. A stream flows through the wet woodland, creating a small pool. Surfaced paths lead through the reserve to Sandwell Valley Country Park.

Legend has it that the unusual name, Sot's Hole, originates from the alcoholic adventures of an eighteenth-century local publican by the name of Richard Reeves,

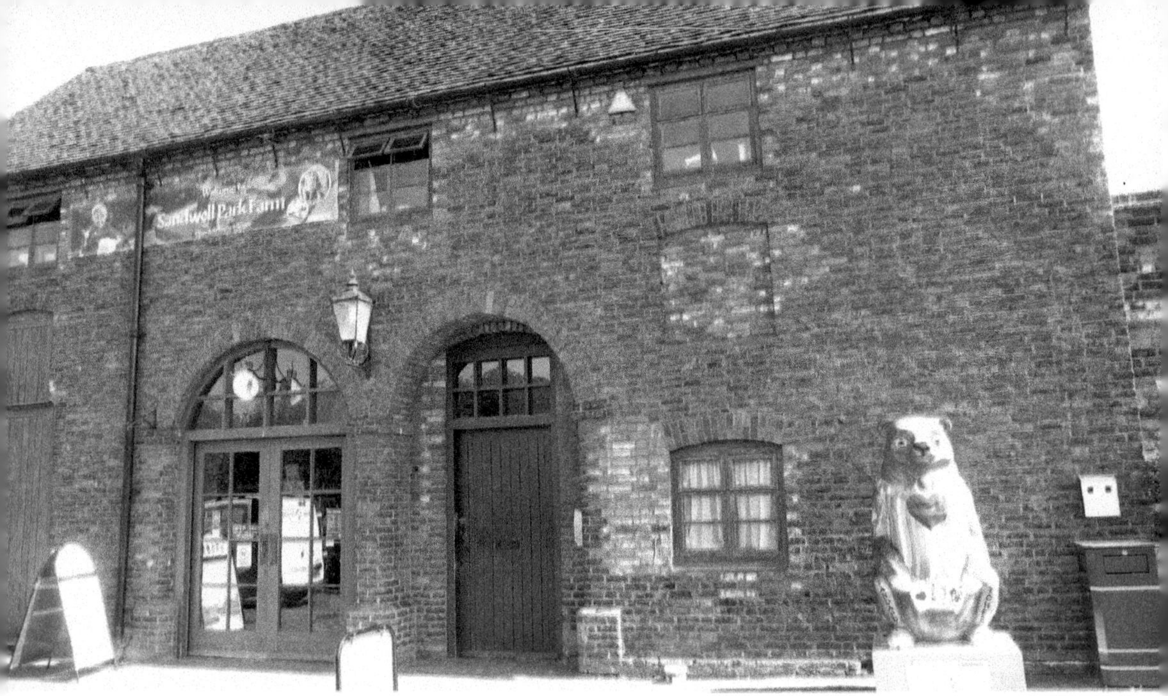

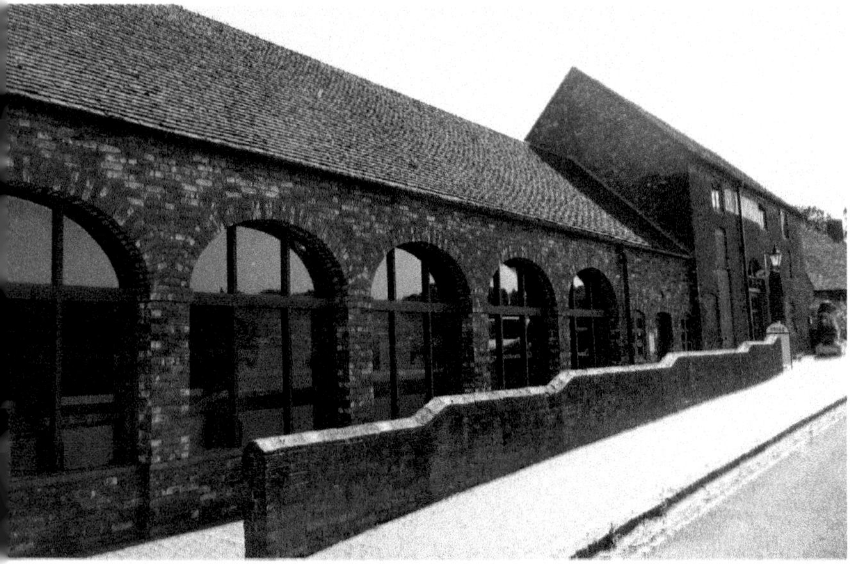

Above and left: Sandwell Park Farm.

landlord of the Bear & Ragged Staff in Church Vale, who liked a drink or ten, so locals called him 'the old sot'. His customers were heavy drinkers who used to relieve themselves in the nearby woods.

The Friends of Sot's Hole group, aided by Sandwell Valley Naturalist Club, are uncovering more of the woodland's background,

Sot's Hole is located on a fault line, and this steep-sided depression splits the reserve in two. Originally there were also coal seams. Evidence of Bronze Age settlers comes from the discovery of a flint mound and a burnt mound, i.e. a heap of stones and charcoal.

The reserves' two pools used to supply water to the mills that once lined the banks of the River Tame, producing iron for all manner of objects including nails and buckles.

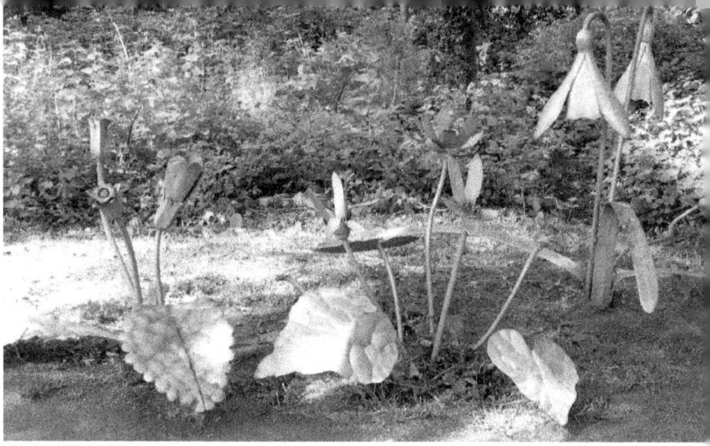

Sculpture, Sandwell Valley Country Park.

Bronze Age tools have been discovered on the site, as well as evidence of cooking and/or bathing. Radiocarbon dating has put one item as being from *c.* 1100 BC.

The reserve is laced with pathways, and there is a visitor centre offering refreshments, souvenirs and bric-a-brac. There are water pools, wild flowers and birds in abundance.

Sot's Hole is located on Church Vale/Dagger Lane, off Hallam Street, West Bromwich, B71 4DD. The entrance is via a kissing gate. Parking is available at the visitor car park, Eaton Valley Primary School, which is just a few metres from the main entrance. For further information visit www.sotshole.co.uk. Tel: 0121 588 6154 or 0121 569 3070.

19. The Manor House, West Bromwich

The Manor House Museum is a Grade I listed black-and-white timber-framed building built around the 1270s by Richard de Marnham, with additions and alterations in the fifteenth and sixteenth centuries. By the 1950s the buildings were in such a dilapidated state that demolition seemed inevitable. Fortunately West Bromwich Corporation stepped in and saved this unique historic property, commissioning welcome restoration work. In the 1960s brewers Ansells took over the tenancy, making extensive renovations before opening the hall as an upmarket pub/restaurant – and very nice it was.

The property is now managed by Sandwell Museum Service, who open it for special events and activities. There are free guided tours on Sundays from the end of July to mid-September (check out the museum's website for more details).

Of the original living-quarters complex only the Great Hall remains. However, there is still much to see. Successive occupants of the hall made alterations, adding to and extending the buildings over the centuries. The two-storey gatehouse was added around 1600. The moat was mostly filled in during the 1700s.

If it's ghosts and ghouls you want then this is the place for you. There's loads of them, plus other scary things such as murder, grave robbing and insanity.

The council has great future plans, including upgrading facilities such as toilets, reception and catering. Address: Hall Green Road, West Bromwich, B71 2EA.

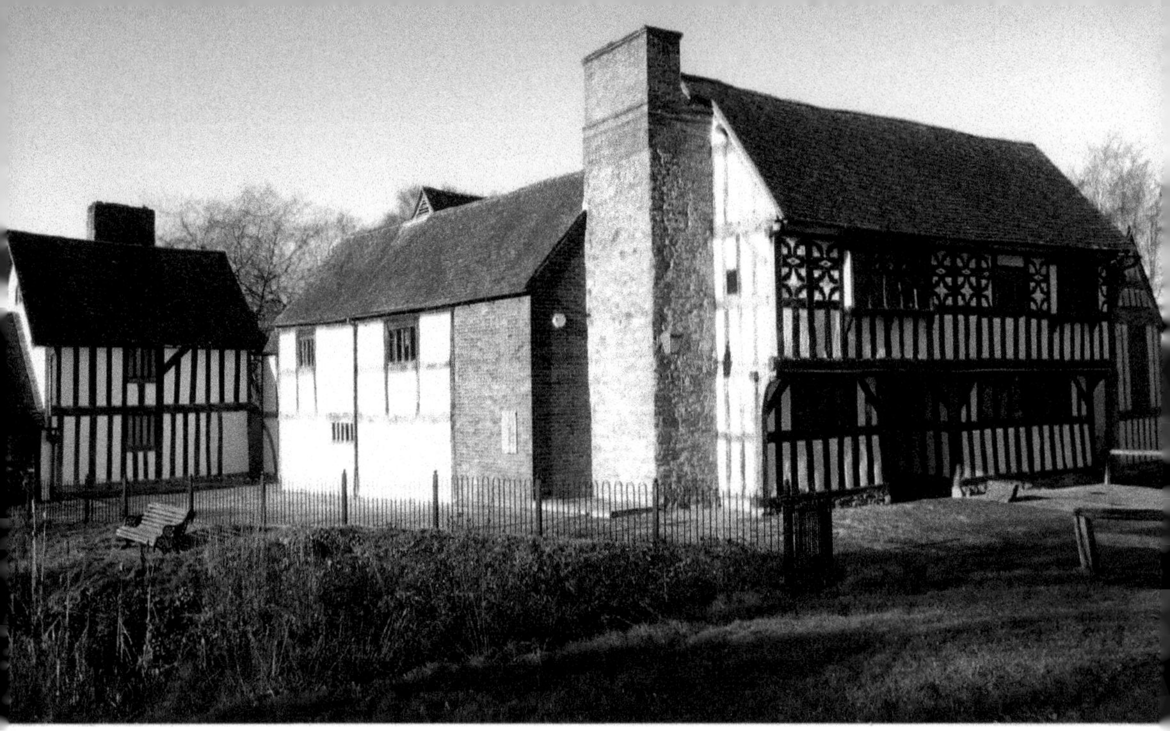

Above and below left and right: The Manor House, West Bromwich.

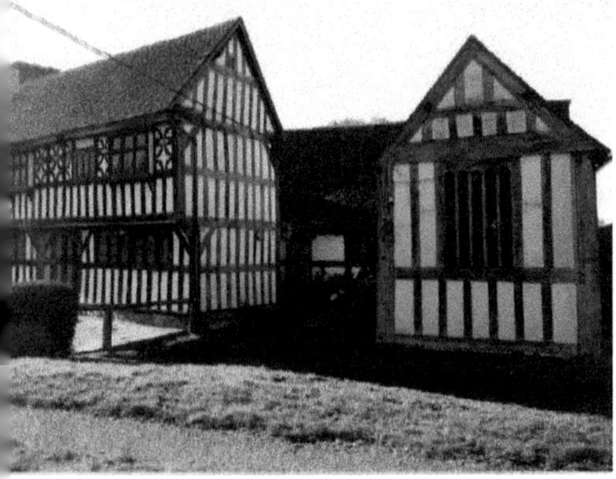

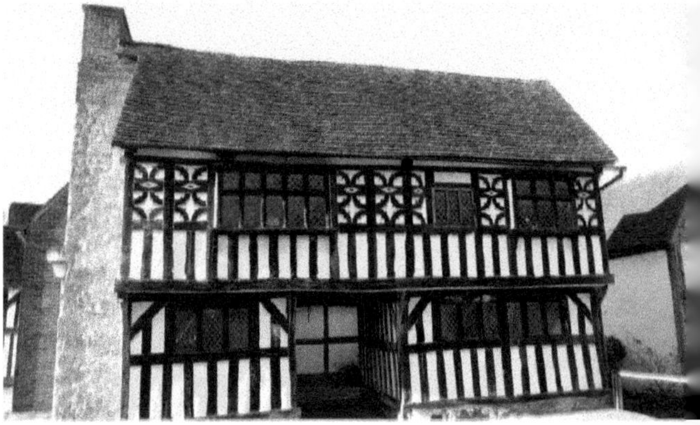

20. Sheepwash Urban Park, Horseley Heath

Sheepwash Urban Park in Horseley Heath is part of the Black Country Urban Forest. Several pools are spread over 96 acres (39 ha), with grassland, young woodland, streams and marshes bordering the River Tame (Oldbury arm). It is a haven for waders, wildfowl, and many other species of bird. It's also a popular place for anglers. The site is on reclaimed land, developed in the 1980s, previously used as a brickworks and as a waste tip.

There's a great leaflet about the Black Country Urban Forest that includes a number of Health Walks: available online or from Groundwork Black Country, Groundwork Environment Centre, Dolton Way, Tipton, DY4 9AL. Tel: 0121 530 5500.

Entrances are situated on Sheepwash Lane, John's Lane and Anne Close. There is limited roadside parking.

Check out www.groundwork.org.uk.

21. Steward Aqueduct, Smethwick

The Grade II listed Steward Aqueduct (sometimes called Stewart Aqueduct) in Smethwick is a truly marvellous site. There is a canal with another canal over that, then a railway line over that, and finally the M5 Motorway bridging the lot – 200 years of British transport history in one place. The Stewart Aqueduct carrying the new main line canal was built in 1829 by world-famous engineer Thomas Telford and sits above the earlier 1770 Old Main Line Birmingham Canal of James Brindley. Construction is brick with sandstone dressings.

Address: Rolfe Street, Warley, B68 2AF.

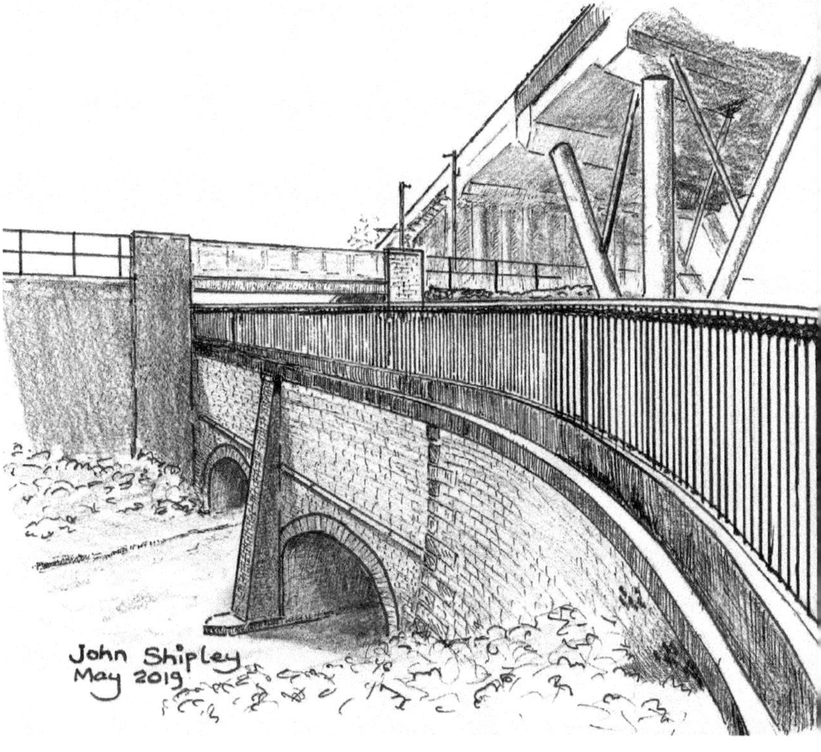

Unique Steward Aqueduct, Smethwick. (Pen and ink drawing by John Shipley)

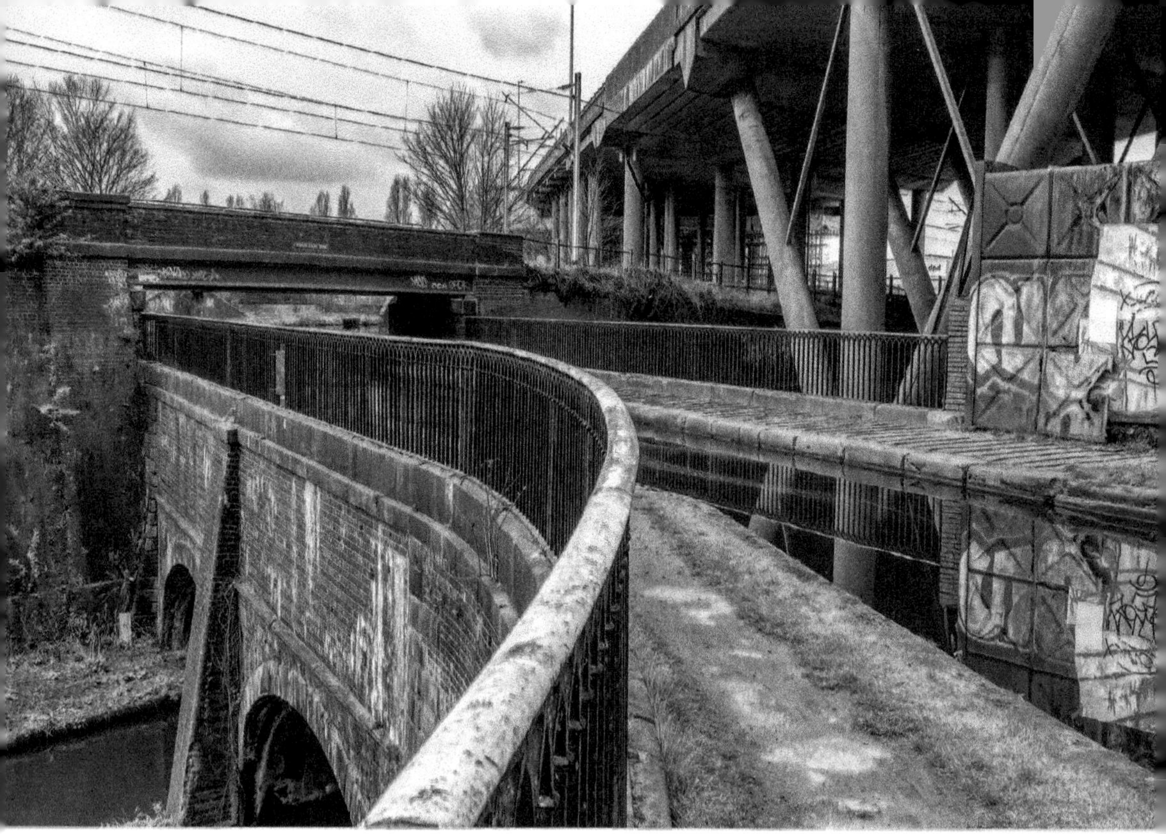

Above: Unique Steward Aqueduct, Smethwick. (Courtesy of Phil Wild)

Below: Engine Arm Aqueduct, Smethwick. (Courtesy of Phil Wild)

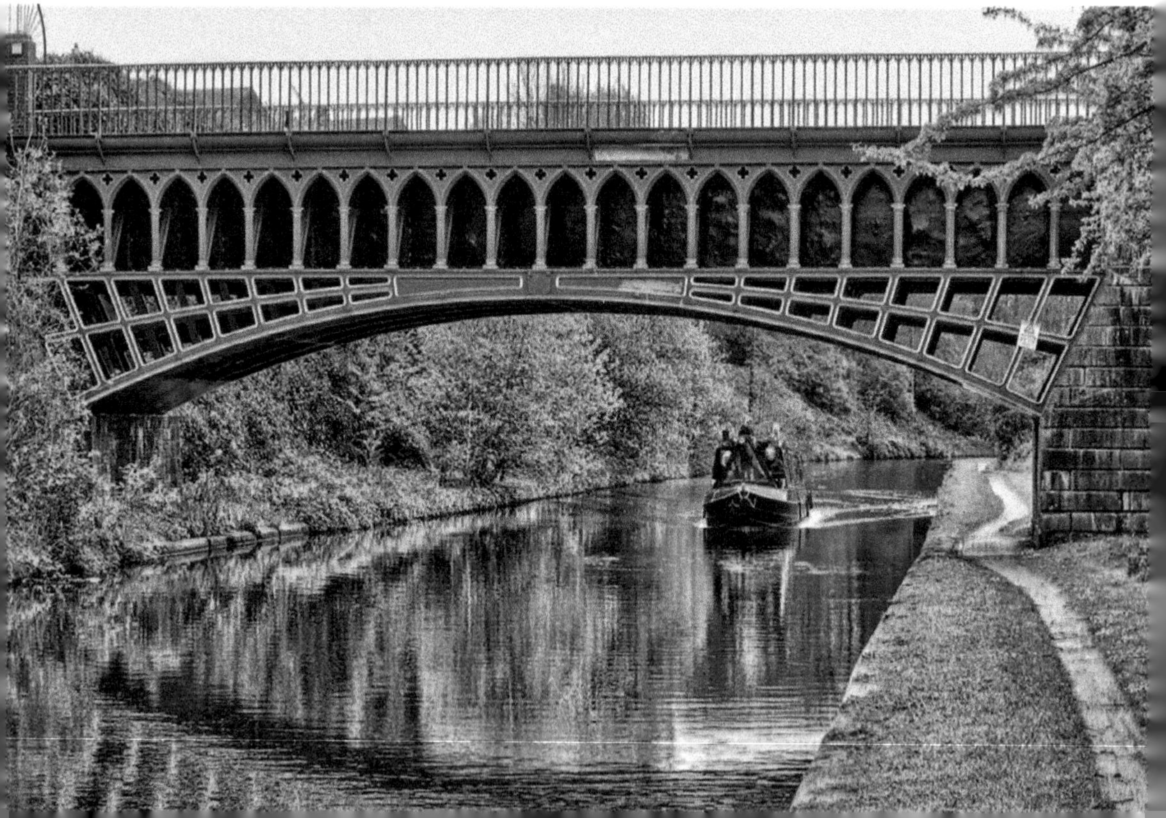

22. Engine Arm Aqueduct, Smethwick

The Grade II listed and Scheduled Ancient Monument Engine Arm Aqueduct in Smethwick is one of a number of beautiful canal bridges in the area. It was built by the legendary engineer Thomas Telford in 1825 to carry a water feeder from Edgbaston Reservoir (formerly known as Rotton Park Reservoir), crossing the New Main Line of the Birmingham Canal. Situated between Galton Bridge and Smethwick junction, the aqueduct has a single span of 52 feet (16 metres) and 8 feet (2.4 metres) wide. Each of the towpaths on either side are 4 feet 4 inches (1.32 metres) wide. The structure consists of a cast-iron trough manufactured by Horseley Ironworks in Great Bridge.

The Grade I listed Galton Bridge, spanning the BCN New Main Line canal, was built by Thomas Telford in 1829 and when it was built the single 151-feet span was the longest in the world. Galton Valley Canal Heritage Centre is to be found in Brasshouse Lane, Smethwick, West Midlands, B66 1BA, Tel: 0121 558 8195.

Spanning the BCN Old Main Line Birmingham Canal not far from the above two aqueducts is the Grade II listed Smeaton's Summit Bridge, carrying Roebuck Lane over the cutting. It was built by John Smeaton in 1788–99 to solve the difficult problem of getting water to the highest point of James Brindley's 1770 canal, which had six locks up to the 491-foot- (150-metre-) high summit and six locks down. Smeaton reduced this to three locks on either side by lowering the height of the cutting to 472 feet (144 metres).

Galton Bridge, Smethwick. (Courtesy of Phil Wild)

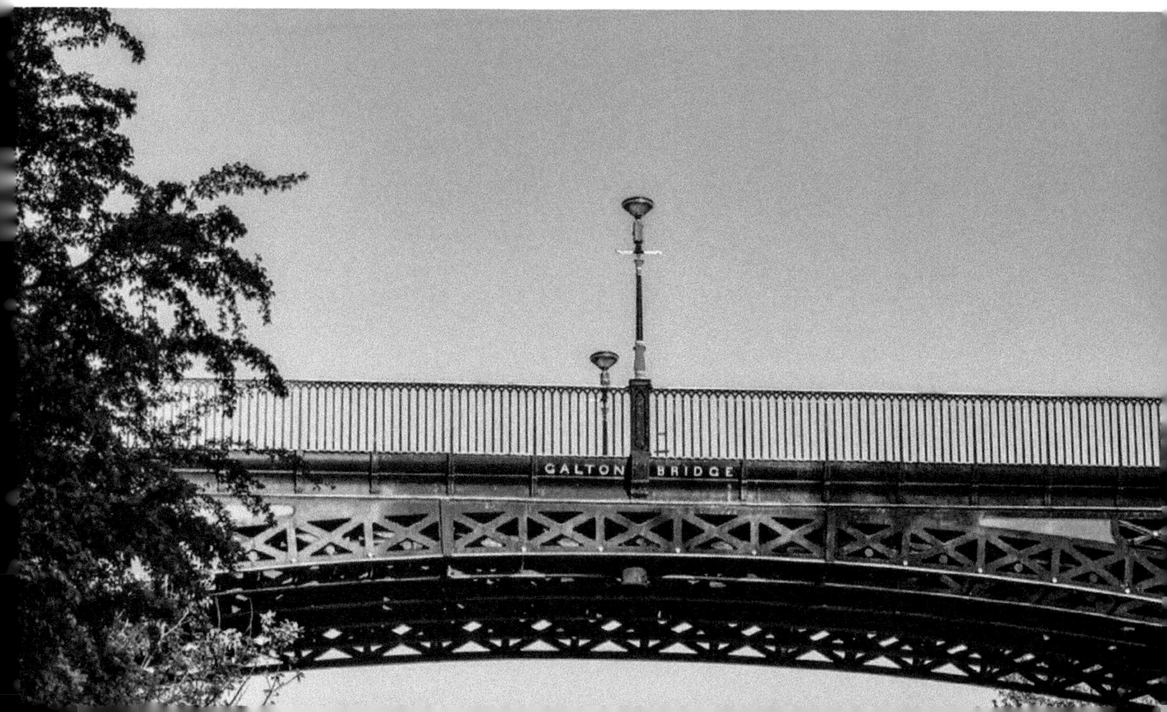

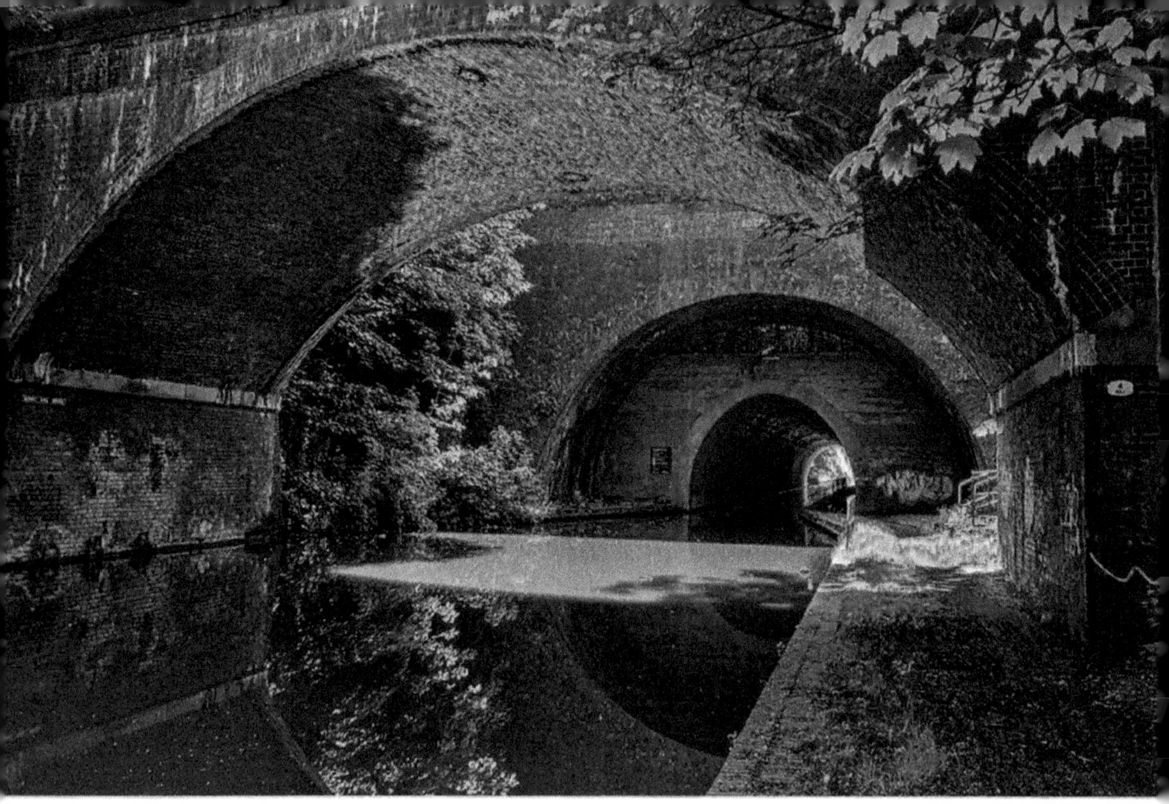

Summit Rail Bridge, Roebuck Lane, Smethwick. (Courtesy of Phil Wild)

23. Ethelfleda Terrace and St Bartholemew's Church, Wednesbury

Ethelfleda Terrace, adjacent to St Batholemew's Parish Church on Church Hill in Wednesbury, holds many secrets from the time of the lady after whom this narrow thoroughfare is named. Her name was, of course, Æthelflæd, Lady of the Mercians (Myrcna hlædige), a true warrior queen in every sense of the word. She was the daughter of King Alfred the Great of Wessex and was married to Æthelred of Mercia. In the West Midlands in *c.* AD 916 she constructed fortifications against the Danish invaders at Wednesbury, Bridgnorth, Tamworth, Stafford and Warwick. Æthelflæd was born around 870 and died on 12 June 918, having ruled Mercia alone since AD 911 following the death of her husband. The Saxons knew Wednesbury as Wodensborough after Woden, the god of war. A lot of local folks call it Wedgebury.

Unfortunately there is no surface evidence left of any fortification created by Æthelflæd or anyone else before or since; however, excavations in 2008 along St Mary's Road, which runs at almost right angles to Ethelfleda Terrace, revealed the remains of a large ditch, which generally follows the hill's contours, believed to date from much earlier than the early medieval period, and possibly part of a large Iron Age hill fort. This discovery raises the possibility that the lady upgraded an earlier fortification, probably a ditch or ditches crowned with an earthwork rampart surmounted by a wooden palisade. When I was a boy locals reckoned that Wednesbury once had a castle and that it stood on the summit of Church Hill, where today stands St Bartholemew's Church.

Wednesbury is the disputed scene of two ancient battles, where according to the Anglo-Saxon Chronicle in AD 592 at the battle of Woden's Burg there was great slaughter where Ceawlin, King of Wessex, was driven out. His opponents, it has been suggested, were Britons. In various versions of the Chronicle the site of the battle is stated as being Woddesbeorge, although another version mentions Wodensbeorge. There's also one that calls the place Wodnesbeorge, and one more that says Wodnesbeorh. The most credible for me is the version in which Henry of Huntingdon in his Chronicle says the battle was at Wednesburie. The second battle was in AD 715, when King Ceolred of Mercia and King Ine of Wessex fought out the Battle of Woden's Burge, also known as the Battle of Woden's Hill, on the same site as the previous battle. The alternative location for both battles is believed to be Adam's Grave near Alton in Wiltshire; however, my preference is Wednesbury as I feel that later historians have followed blindly the incorrect conclusions of earlier historians.

Below left: Ethelfleda Gardens, Ethelfleda Terrace, Wednesbury.

Below right: St Bartholemew's Church, Church Hill, Wednesbury.

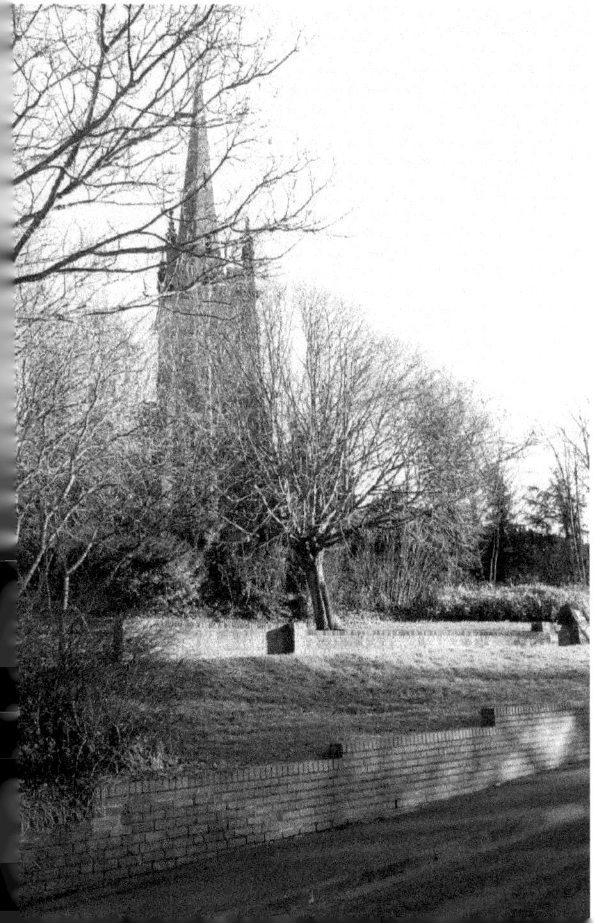

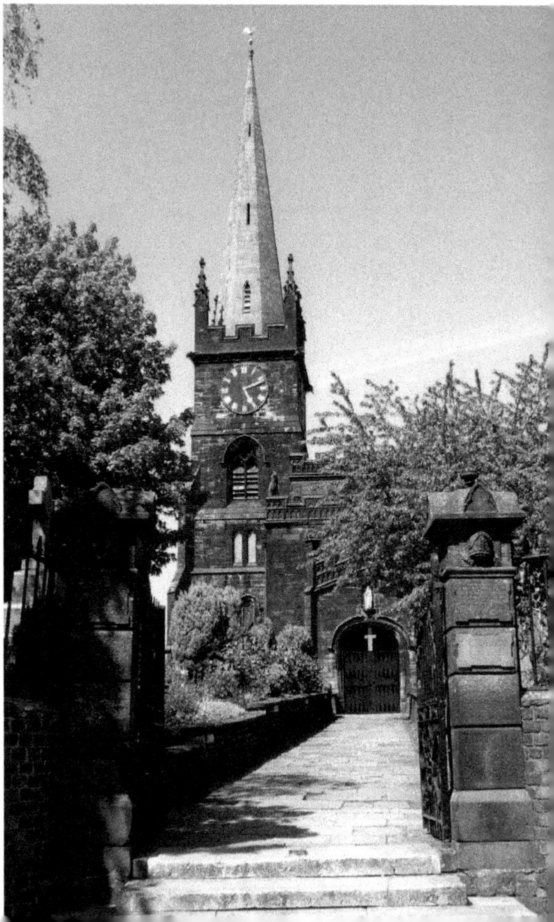

The first written mention of St Bartholemew's Church on the top of Church Hill in Wednesbury was in 1088. The present Grade II listed church has medieval origins, standing on the site of an earlier thirteenth-century stone church, with alterations and additions dating from the late fifteenth or early sixteenth century, and substantially enlarged in Victorian times. The lofty position of St Bart's, as it is known locally, affords an extensive prospect over the surrounding countryside. Inside this imposing structure is a marvellous carved pulpit dated 1611, there are also medieval furnishings, and impressive stained-glass windows by William Kempe. In 1757 the tower was restored and the topmost 16 feet was rebuilt. The church is recorded in King John's Plea Rolls for 1210/11.

In 1743 Wednesbury took on a new fame when Methodist preachers and founders John Wesley and his brother Charles came to the town to establish their new religious thinking, and by all accounts they were made welcome and treated fairly. However, on a subsequent visit John Wesley was almost killed when a mob, outnumbering his supporters, rioted. The scene turned ugly, but eventually calm descended and order was restored. John Wesley visited the town on thirty-three occasions between 1743 and 1790, during which time Methodism grew and became the calling of many. A plaque set into a stone on the High Bullen commemorates his visits. By 1791, the year of his death, there were in the region of 100,000 Methodists. John Wesley famously preached from a horse mounting block situated on the High Bullen, which was relocated, and for many years stood outside the old Spring Head Methodist chapel. The mounting block is now to be found at the Wesley Centre, Wednesbury Central Methodist Church, Spring Head, Wednesbury.

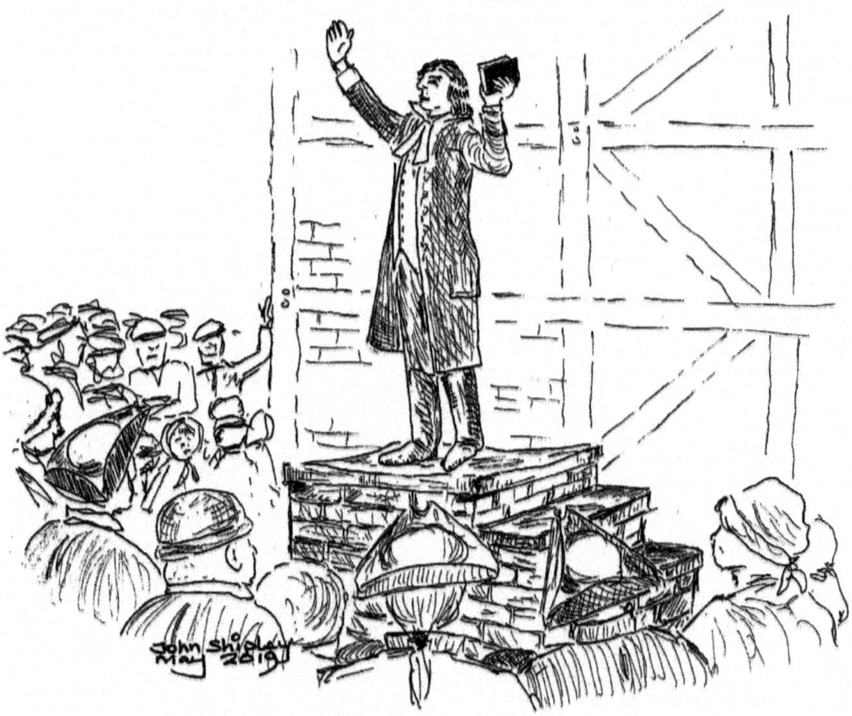

John Wesley preaching in Wednesbury. (Pen and ink drawing by John Shipley)

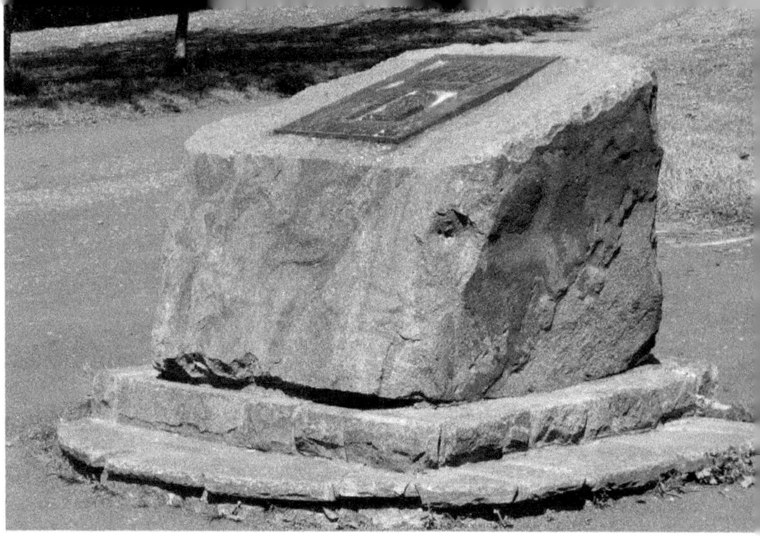

Plinth commemorating John Wesley's preaching visits to Wednesbury.

24. Ye Olde Leathern Bottel, Wednesbury

This timber-framed black-and-white inn is one of the oldest in the West Midlands, if not the oldest. The sign on the wall tells us that Wednesbury's Ye Olde Leathern Bottel was established in 1510. Tucked away on Vicarage Road and the corner of Handley Street, it's a quaint watering hole that's well worth a visit. Years 'agoo' they used to serve a great pint of Highgate Mild.

Along with stacks of other inns the Bottel maintains the legend that Dick Turpin, the notorious eighteenth-century highwayman, stopped off here for a pint and to

Ye Olde Leathern Bottel, Wednesbury.

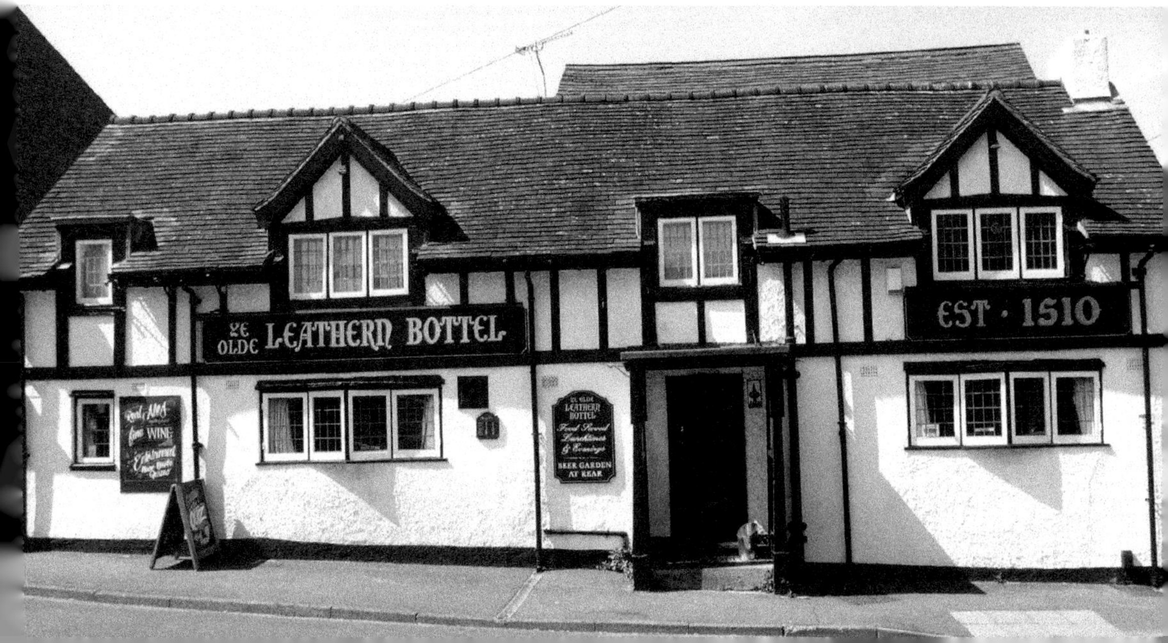

water his horse. The legend makes no mention of Black Bess, so we have to assume it was indeed Turpin's legendary fiery black steed that he was riding at the time. Apparently the outlaw was on his way from London to York, and in fact in those days the main road to Walsall passed the front of the inn, although travelling via Wednesbury and Walsall would require quite a detour, but remember Turpin didn't have satnav.

Address: No. 40 Vicarage Road, Wednesbury, WS10 9DW. Tel: 0121 505 0230.

25. Cobbs Engine House and Chimney, Warrens Hall Local Nature Reserve and Bumble Hole Local Nature Reserve

At the heart of Windmill End in Netherton is a wonderful reclaimed green space consisting of Warrens Hall Local Nature Reserve, which is partly in Sandwell, and Bumble Hole Local Nature Reserve inside the Dudley boundary. The area includes a number of important landmarks of our industrial past: Cobb's Engine House (a farmer named Cobb once owned the land), Timber Gallows Crane (not there at the moment), and the intriguingly named Blow Cold Bank Colliery Spoil Heap.

Cobb's Engine House, or, to use its official name, Windmill End Pumping Station, is a Grade II listed Scheduled Ancient Monument. It was built around 1831/1836 to house a stationary steam-powered Newcomen-style Engine designed to pump water from a 525-feet- (160-metres) deep mine shaft at Windmill End Colliery. Reputedly, every day, more than 420,000 gallons (1.6 million litres) of water were pumped into the local Dudley No. 2 canal system. A specially built railway line was used to bring coal to power the engine. Originally a three-storey construction, sadly the roof has not survived the ravages of time. The chimney that stands alongside is 95 feet (29 metres) tall, tapering from 11 feet 6 inches (3.5 metres) square at its base to 4 feet (1.2 metres) square at the top. The pump ceased operating in 1928, and two years later was taken to America to be housed in the Henry Ford Museum in Dearborn, Michigan. The steep mound east of the chimney is in fact a spoil heap, affording great views from its summit, made up of mining waste dug out from the Blow Cold Bank Colliery pits. The section of Dudley No. 2 canal passing through the reserve originally included the Bumble Hole Loop, an irregular semicircular arc, now much shortened due to subsidence, and which linked to the Boshboil Arm. A straighter section was subsequently constructed. At the point where the Boshboil Arm meets the newer section of canal a new section was created to link to the Wolverhampton & Birmingham Canal, passing through the 3,027-yard- (2,768-metre-) long Netherton Tunnel, built between 1855 and 1858. The portal

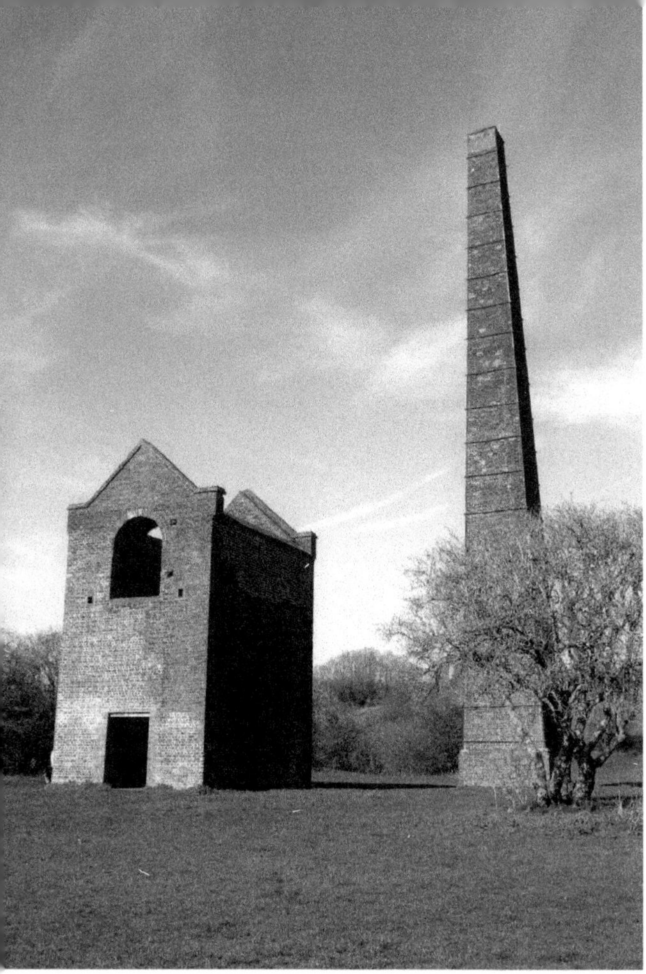

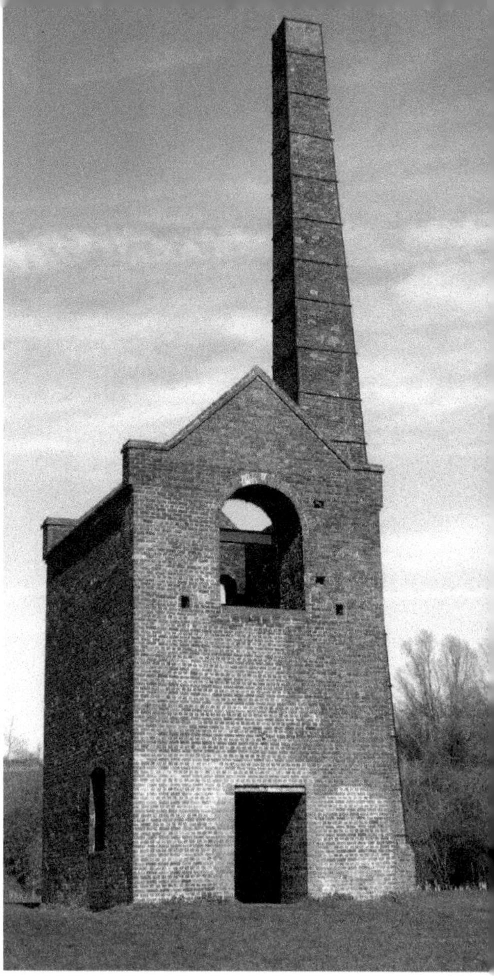

Above left and right: Cobb's Engine House, Bumble Hole.

Below: Bumble Hole.

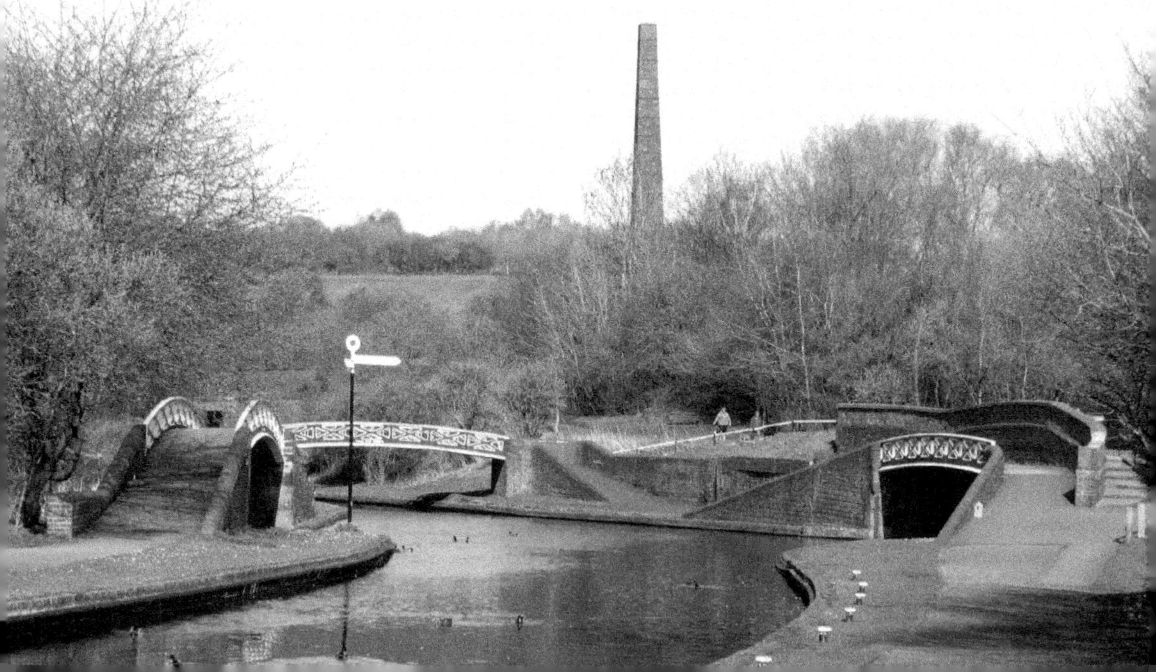

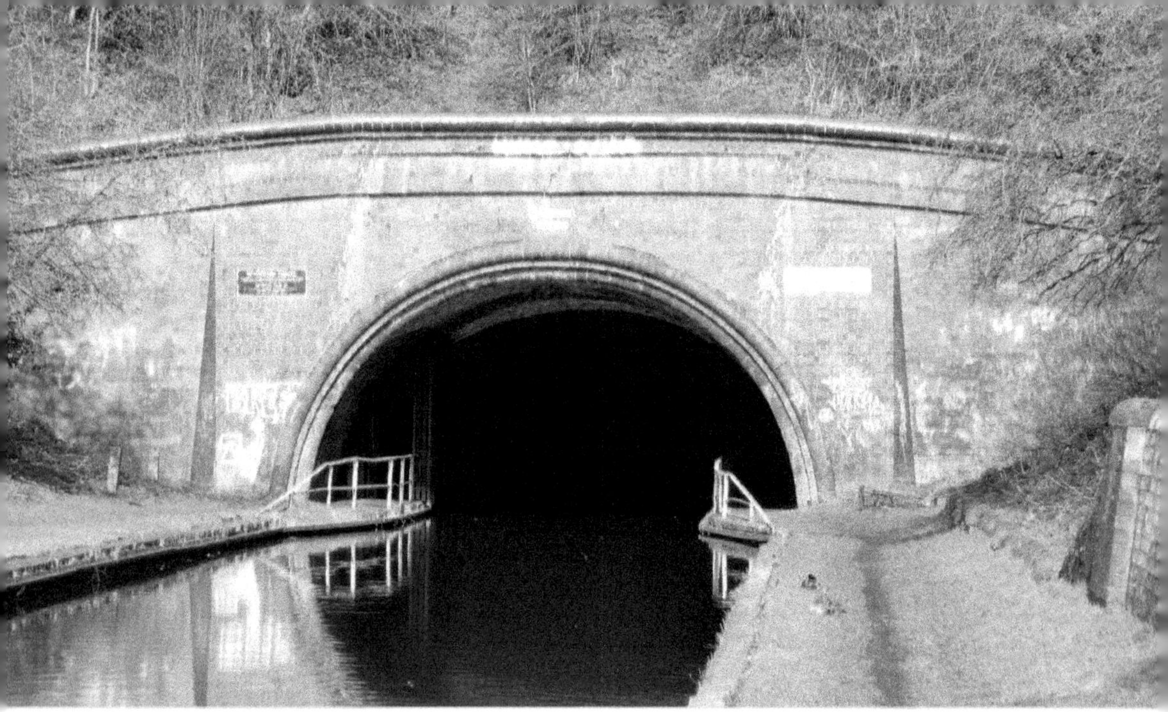

The Grade II listed entrance to the Netherton Tunnel.

around the entrance is Grade II listed. This was reputedly the last great tunnel to be built in the canal age. It's also the widest because it has a towpath on both sides of the canal, so no need for 'legging'.

Timber Gallows Crane, another Scheduled Ancient Monument, used to be found here, a rare design that is believed to be the last of its kind in the country, and was estimated to be able to lift 20 tons. It ceased working in the 1970s and is now away undergoing restoration.

The two reserves have some great spots to visit with some great names: Boshboil Pond, also known as the Red Pool because of the reddish/orange colour of the man-made island in its centre. The colour is created by the chemical reaction from a mixture of oxygen, water, and oxidised metal. Bumble Hole Lake today is a haven for waterfowl; however, it is really an eighteenth-century man-made clay pit, the clay from which was used to make pottery, bricks and also to line furnaces. The distinctive dark-blue colour of the bricks, known locally as 'tocky' bricks (Black Country spake fer 'sticky'), comes from the firing of Staffordshire clay. Hard Dolerite (known locally as 'Rowley Rag') was mined at Hailstone Quarry. There are a number of lovely sweeping arc cast-iron bridges in the reserve.

The origin of the name Bumble Hole is a little bit controversial. One legend has it that a huge steam hammer once operated from the once dry bottom of the clay pit, making a 'bum-hul' sound, i.e. bum-hul in th'ole, morphing into Bumble Hole – sounds a bit tenuous to say the least. Another is that the name is derived from the Middle English word describing the humming of a bumblebee. Either way it has nothing to do with Mr Bumble of *Oliver Twist* fame.

Friends of the Bumble Hole & Warren Hall Local Nature Reserves, a volunteer organisation, came together in May 1993, officially forming in 1994. The reserve hosts the annual Black Country Boating Festival every September.

There is a visitor centre that is open most mornings, but it's best to check to make sure. Tel: 01384 814100 and 814189. Address: St Peter's Road, Dudley, DY2 9HB.

26. Bishop Asbury Cottage, Great Barr

This small unassuming cottage dating from the eighteenth century was the boyhood home of Francis Asbury, a young man who went on to become the first American Methodist bishop. Francis was born in Handsworth in August 1745, and lived in the cottage after his parents moved there when he was one year old until he was aged twenty-six. He worked as a blacksmith and developed his belief in the Methodism, attending the Methodist church in Wednesbury. He left home for America around 1771 at the behest of John Wesley himself, to spread the word of Methodism. Bishop Francis Asbury died in Spotsylvania in 1816. He is buried in Baltimore, Maryland.

The cottage is furnished in period style, and contains memorabilia and information on Francis Asbury's life in West Bromwich and America, plus information about Methodism, with links to the life and times of John Wesley. The cottage has become a Mecca for American Methodists visiting the UK. There are no facilities or parking on site, but there is limited parking available next door on the car park of the Malt Shovel public house (best to ask to use it).

Address: Newton Road, Great Barr, B43 6HN. For more information check the website www.sandwell.gov.uk. Tel: 0121 556 0683.

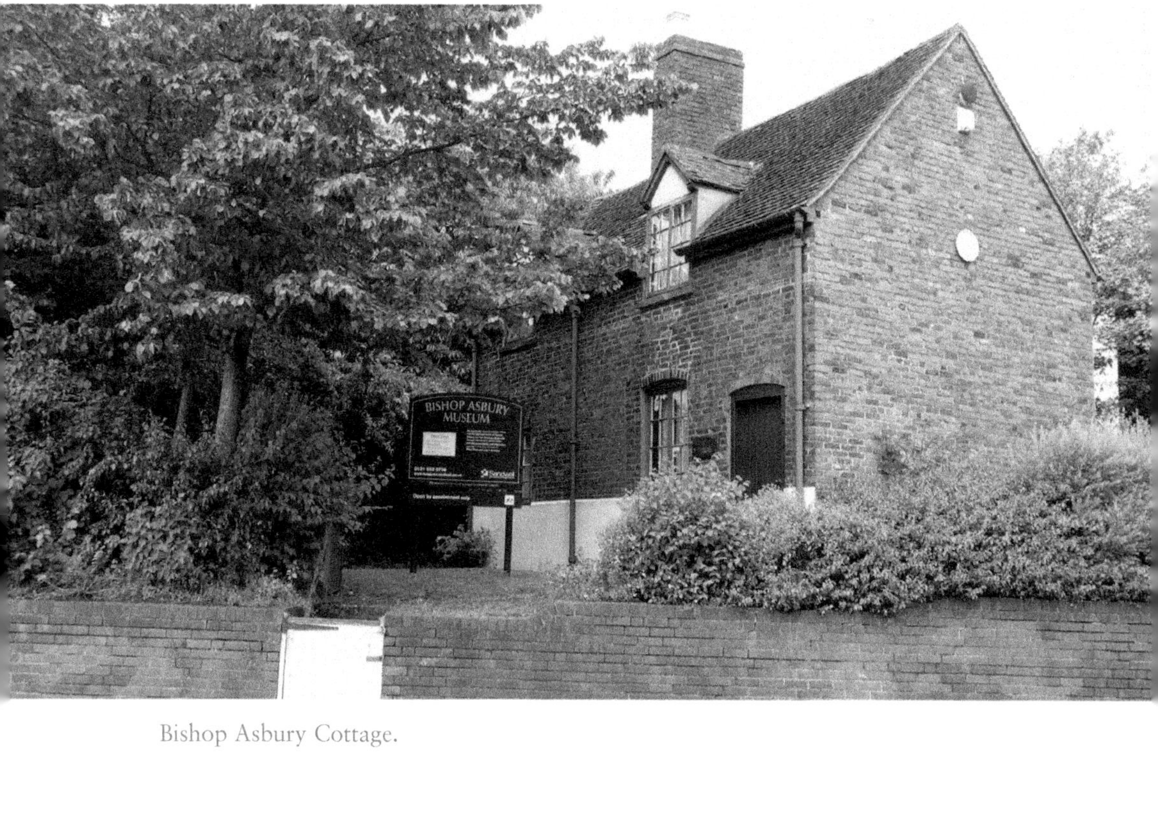

Bishop Asbury Cottage.

27. Haden Hill House and Park, Cradley Heath

Standing within 55 acres (22.2 ha) of parkland, Haden Hill House was built in 1878 by George Alfred Haden Haden-Best next to the site of a much earlier house that is known affectionately as the 'Tudor Hall'. The two houses are what one might call posh semi-detatched. The earlier 'Old' Haden Hall, most probably dates from the late 1600s, and was the home of the reasonably well-off yeoman farming Haden family from then until when the new house was built. It has been suggested that the family can trace their line back to Norman times, to Ricardo atte Haudene, who was given permission to build a house on a hill in Rowley (Haden Hill). However there appears to be no documentary evidence to support this. George Alfred Best (then residing at Corngreaves Hall) inherited the estate from his uncle Frederick W. G. Barrs in 1877. A condition of this was that he added the name Haden to his, thus he became George Alfred Haden Haden-Best.

Over the centuries the original 'Old' Haden Hall has seen many restorations, rebuilds and fires, but the shell that is left is pleasant to look at.

Following George Alfred's death in 1921 the house and grounds were auctioned, purchased for £8,500, a sum raised by public conscription, to take the house and park into public ownership. Rowley Regis Urban District Council

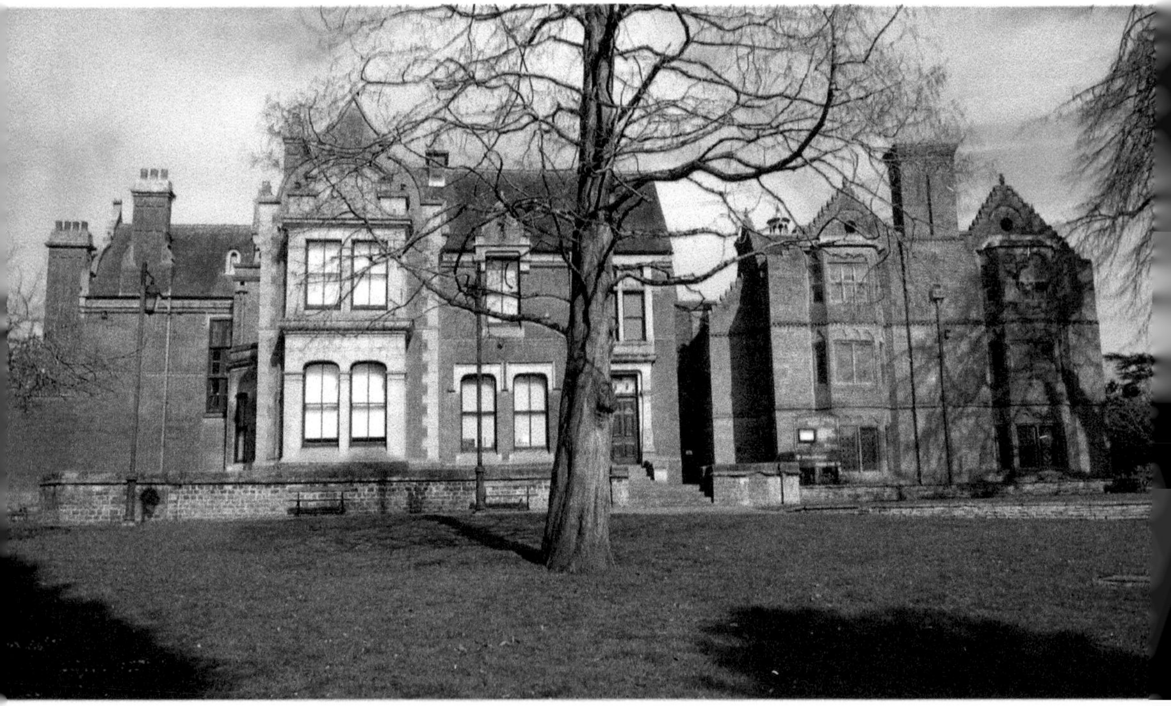

Haden Hill House.

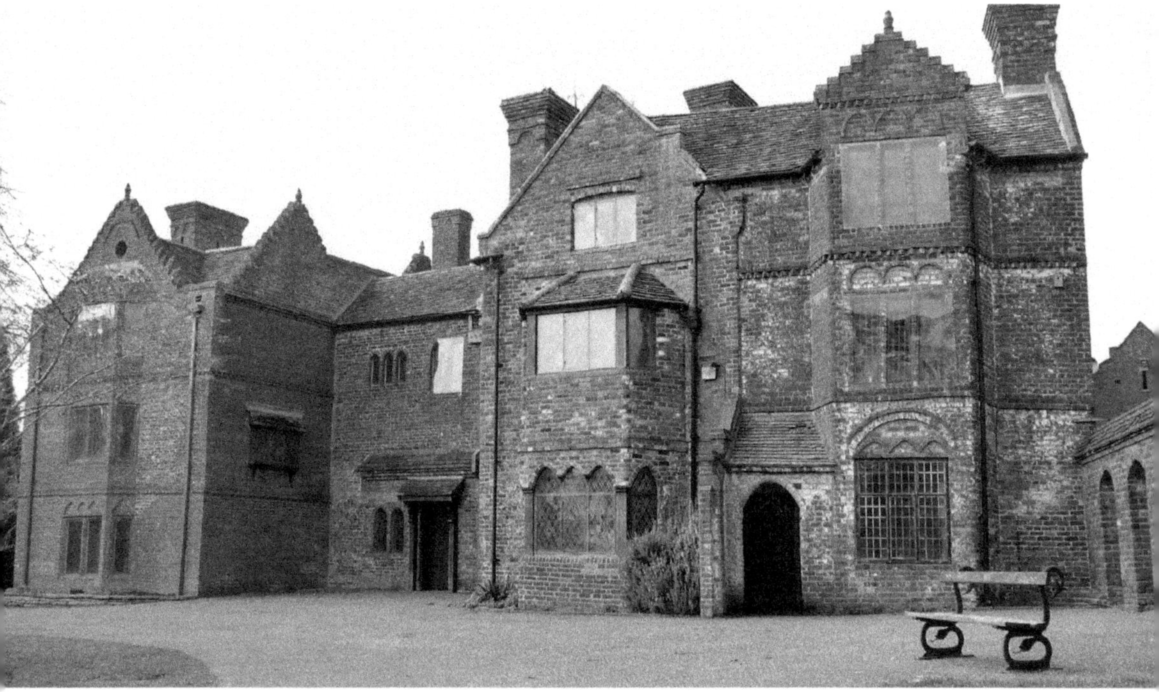

Old Haden Hill House.

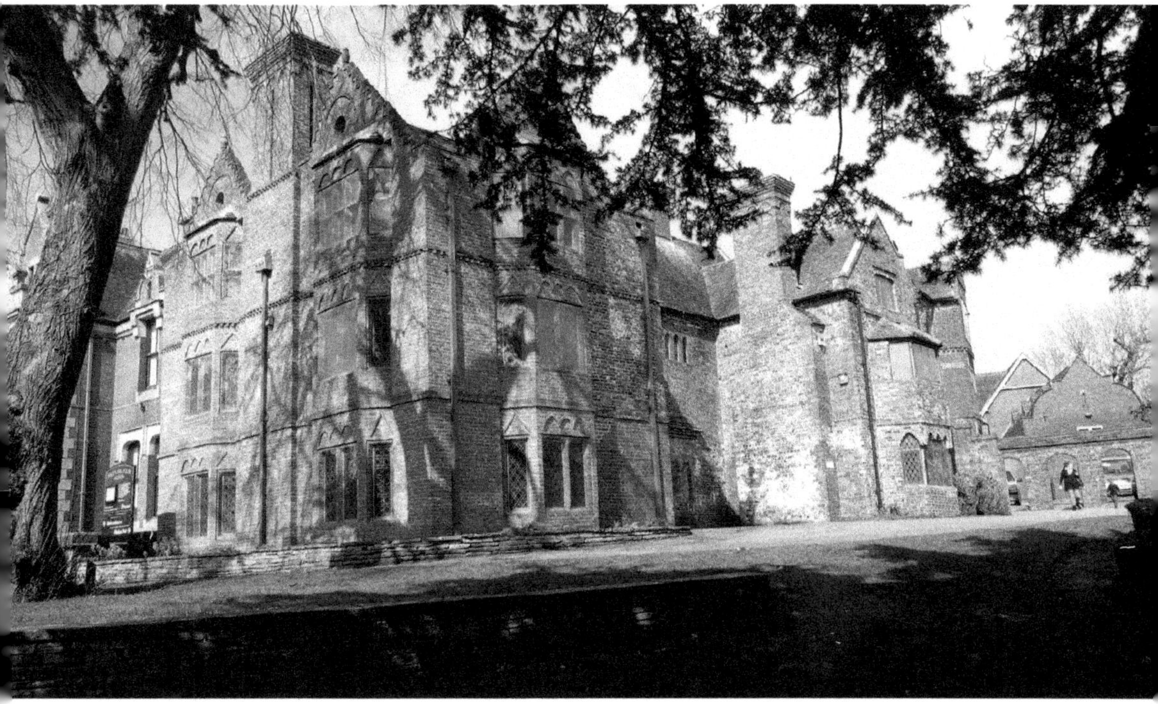

Haden Hill House.

took over the deeds to the property in 1922, and the park opened to the public in October 1922. Sadly both houses fell into disrepair, resulting in the formation of the Haden Hill Preservation Society and the Haden Hill Park Protection Trust. Restoration of the Victorian house began in 1983 and finished in 1989, and was opened to the public later that year. The Victorian house is now a museum, furnished in the style of that time.

Haden Hill Park is a lovely place for a walk or a picnic. There's also a children's play area, sports pitches, an impressive lake, ornamental pools and formal laid out gardens. Enthusiastic bowls and tennis players are also catered for. The park is open daily from 7 a.m. to 8.30 p.m.

Address: Halesowen Road, Cradley Heath, B64 7UJ. However, the entrance is in Lee Road, off Barrs Road.

28. Corngreaves Hall and Corngreaves Nature Reserve

This crenellated Grade II listed building dates from the late eighteenth century, built by local ironmaster James Attwood (uncle of Birmingham's first MP, Thomas Attwood). The hall stands on the site of an earlier building said by some to have been the moated Corngreaves Castle, although there is no evidence of this. Interestingly when the workmen employed to tear down the previous sandstone block structure they reportedly discovered a 'secret' chamber inhabited by two male skeletons dating from the time of the English Civil War. The two men apparently died in mortal combat, each holding a bloodied rusty dagger. A piece of decaying cloth was identified as being part of a Roundhead soldier's uniform. James Attwood is supposed to have had the remains buried in a specially built tomb in the grounds of the hall. Again there is no evidence to support this. Another legend tells of two murders on the site.

The hall lies on the edge of the Corngreaves Nature Reserve, which in turn connects to Haden Hill Park, near the River Stour, which marks the boundary between Sandwell and Dudley, a waterway that once featured many industrial mills along its banks specialising in casting, forging, rolling and slitting metal. All this led to the suspicion that the previous building on the site may have been an old water-driven mill, which would have had a millrace to carry the water necessary to drive the waterwheel, which might be the moat referred to earlier. The hall also once housed the headquarters of the Corngreaves Ironworks, the British Iron Company, then the New British Iron Company until the operations ceased in 1912.

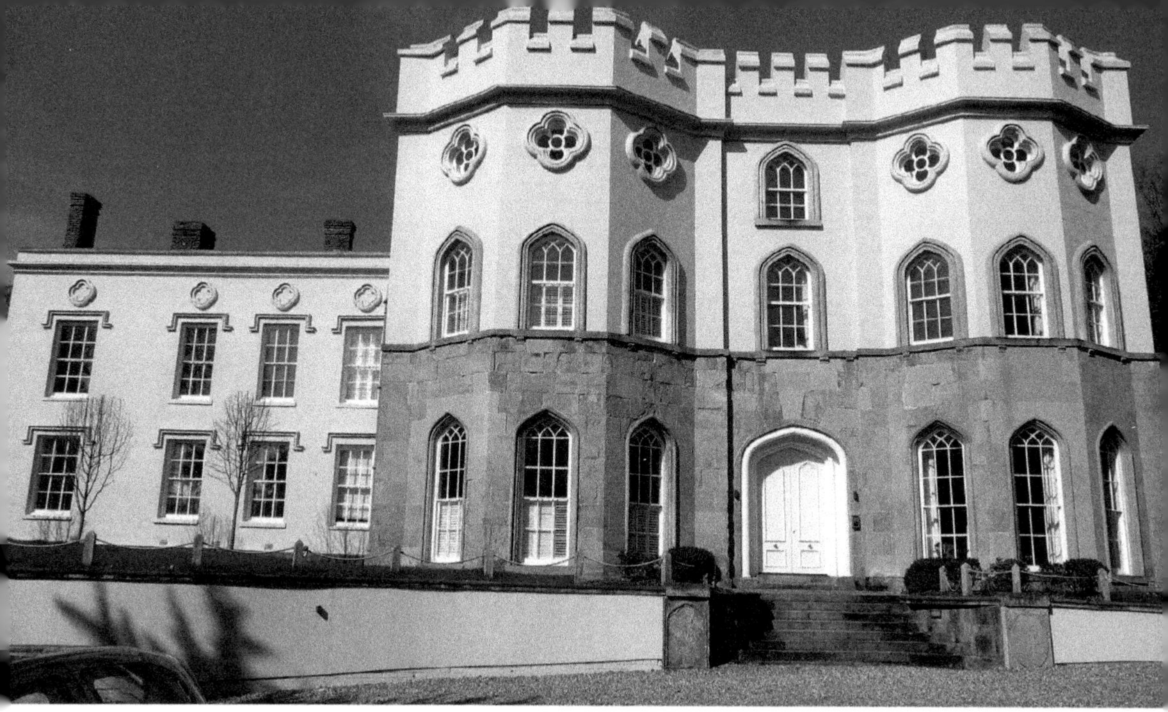

Corngreaves Hall.

Eventually the hall was sold to Rowley Regis Borough Council, but in its time was also used as a Women's temperance home, a golf club, and the place where Steve Winwood's band Traffic rehearsed (saxophonist Chris Wood lived there). It has since been converted into apartments.

The adjacent Corngreaves Nature Reserve is a lovely spot to spend some time outdoors, paths connect the site with Haden Hill Park. Check website www.sandwell.org.uk for details of parking, etc. Address: Corngreaves Road, Cradley Heath, B64 7EA.

29. Warley Woods Park

Situated within the 100 acres of Warley Woods Park is a delightful nine-hole golf course in what were once the grounds of Warley Abbey. However, this was no ancient religious house. It was in fact a Gothic mansion, originally named New Warley Hall, and built in the revival style by Hubert John Barclay Galton, second of the three surviving sons of Birmingham Quaker gunmaker Samuel John Galton Jnr of Barr Hall, Great Barr. Scottish architect Robert Lugar designed the hall, and Hubert Galton took up residence in 1819.

It's likely that the estate of 'Old' Warley Hall, together with its farm, was created following Henry VIII's 1538 Dissolution of the Monasteries, the original Warley Hall being built in the 1500s by a man named Warley. Apparently there are documents relating to the Warley family that date from the reign of Elizabeth I. The Warley's subsequently sold the estate, ownership changing often. In 1792 William Russell sold the estate to Samuel Galton Jnr for £7,300. Galton commissioned renowned landscape architect Humphry Repton to lay out the grounds, including a modest house called Warley Tor. The grounds included an ornamental lake, but this has long since disappeared, plus a Doric Pavillion, demolished in 1906, along with the South Lodge gatehouse. The hall was extended in the 1860s. The Galton family left the hall around 1840, but ownership of the estate stayed in the Galton family until 1928, following the death of Major Hubert George Howard Galton of Hadzor Hall, Droitwich, whose two sons were killed in the First World War. Sadly the building was demolished in 1957.

Warley Woods gained notoriety in June 1919 when it was the scene of the grisly murder of itinerant Chinese labourer Zee Ming Wu, a hard-working man who diligently saved his money with a view to returning to his native land to support his family; his Post Office Savings book containing £240 was stolen in the attack. His hideously battered body was discovered by a boy, Henry Thomas Wilson. Djang Djing Sung, another Chinese labourer, was arrested for the crime, convicted and hanged at Worcester on 3 December 1919 by John Ellis.

In 1999 Warley Woods Community Trust was formed with the aim of retaining the parkland as a public space. This voluntary organisation and registered charity now manage the park, which has benefited from a grant from the Heritage Lottery Fund.

Address: Lightwoods Hill, just off Hagley Road A456, B67 5ED.

30. The Hawthorns, Home of West Bromwich Albion

Home of West Bromwich Albion, the Hawthorns has the distinction of being the highest football ground above sea level in the English football leagues at 551 feet (168 metres). The ground has been the home of West Bromwich Albion since September 1900, the sixth ground used by the club following its formation in 1878. There previous grounds were Cooper's Hill, Dartmouth Park, Bunn's Field (known as the Birches), Four Acres Ground (West Bromwich Dartmouth Cricket Club) and Stoney Lane. The Hawthorns is situated on the border with Handsworth, on a site that was once covered with hawthorn bushes (hence the name). The club signed a lease for the site on 14 May 1900 from the owners, Sandwell Park Colliery, purchasing the freehold in 1913.

West Bromwich Albion played their first match at the Hawthorns on Monday 3 September 1900, in front of 20,104 spectators, drawing 1-1 with Derby County. The goal scorers were Steve Bloomer for the visitors and Chippy Simmons for the Albion.

Address: Birmingham Road, B71 4LF. Website: www.wba.co.uk.

The Wolverhampton Metropolitan Borough Area

The first settlement was founded here by Anglo-Saxon noblewoman Wulfrun or Wulfruna in AD 985. The land, granted to her by charter by her grandfather, Æthelred II (known as the Unready), was called Heatun, which in Anglo-Saxon means 'a high or principle farm or enclosure', hence: Wulfrun's Heaton, which over time morphed into Wolverehamptonia in 1070, and finally into Wolverhampton.

31. Bantock House Museum and Park, Wolverhampton

Surrounded by 48 acres of parkland, the Grade II listed Bantock House is a delightful example of upper-class Edwardian life. Originally the farmhouse of New Merridale Farm, it was built in the 1730s with subsequent remodellings by later owners and tenents. Around the early nineteenth century the building was renamed Merridale House. In 1864 the property was purchased by Scotsman Thomas Bantock, a former canal and railway agent, self-made owner of coal mines (Springfield, Bilston) and ironworks (building boats and wagons at Millfields, Ettingshall), becoming home to him and his wife Mary and their ten children. His son, Albert Baldwin Bantock, who took over the family firm on the death of his father in 1895, was Mayor of Wolverhampton on three occasions, and in 1920 was also High Sheriff of Staffordshire, and Freeman of the Borough in 1926. Albert redesigned the gardens and parkland, and upon his death in 1938, childless, he bequeathed the house and gardens to Wolverhampton Corporation, who in 1940 renamed the house Bantock House in his honour.

Today the informally laid out museum tells the story of the house, some of the people that lived there and other prominent local business families associated with

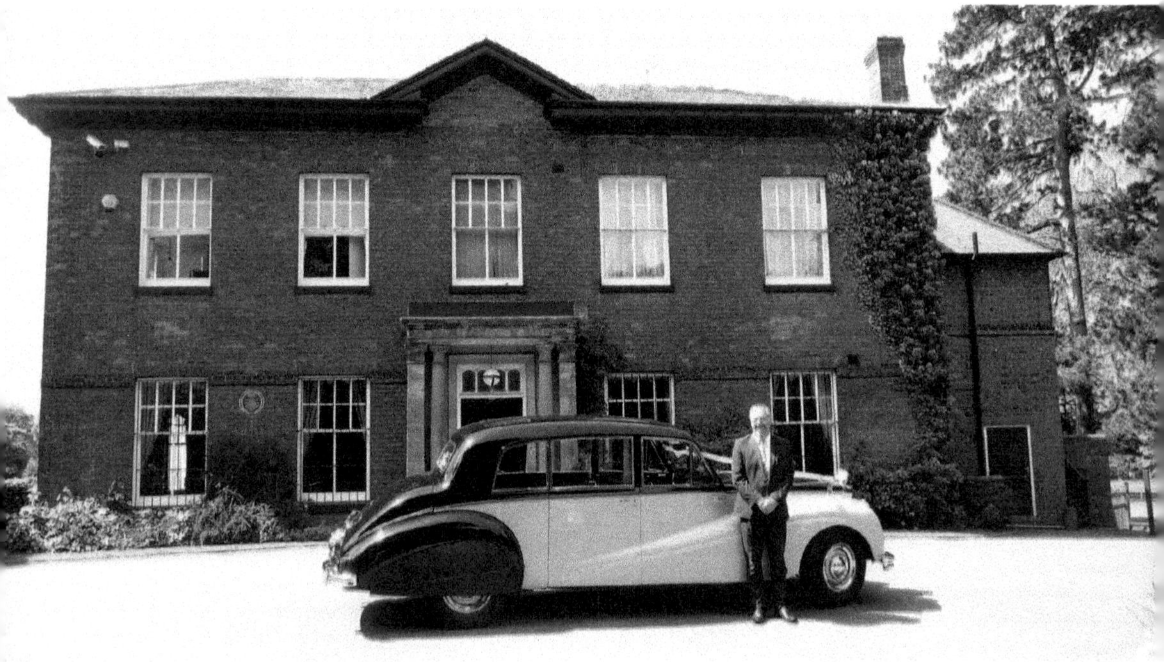

Bantock House. Steve Smith of Elmwood Cars with his classic Armstrong Siddeley limousine. (www.elmwoodcars.co.uk)

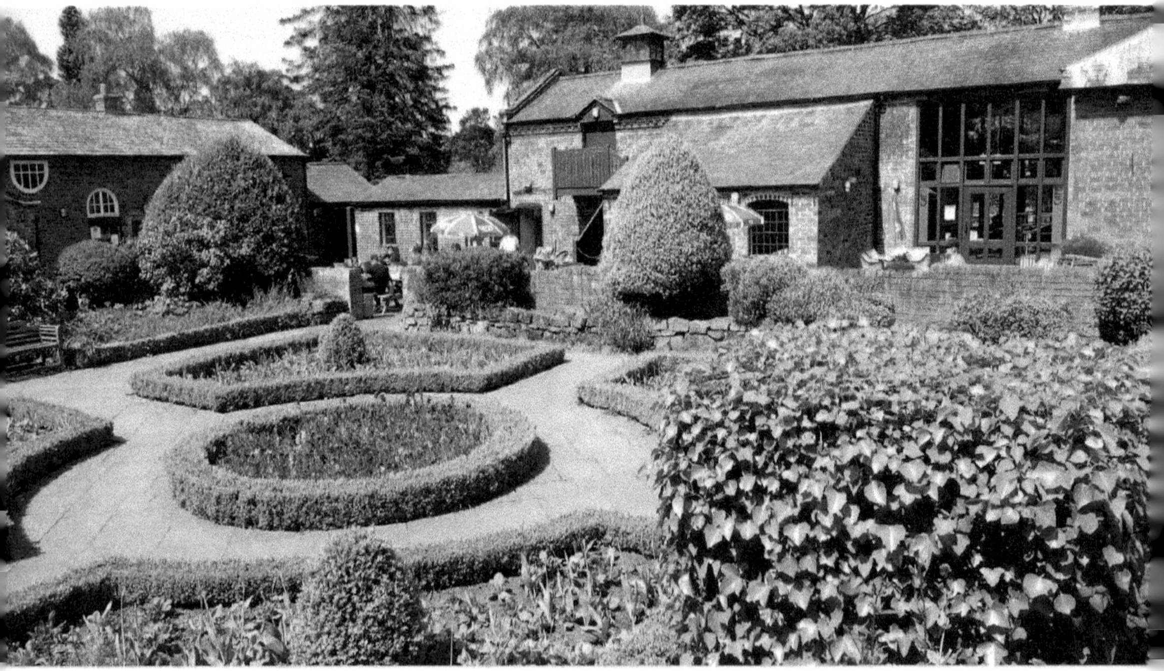

Bantock House courtyard.

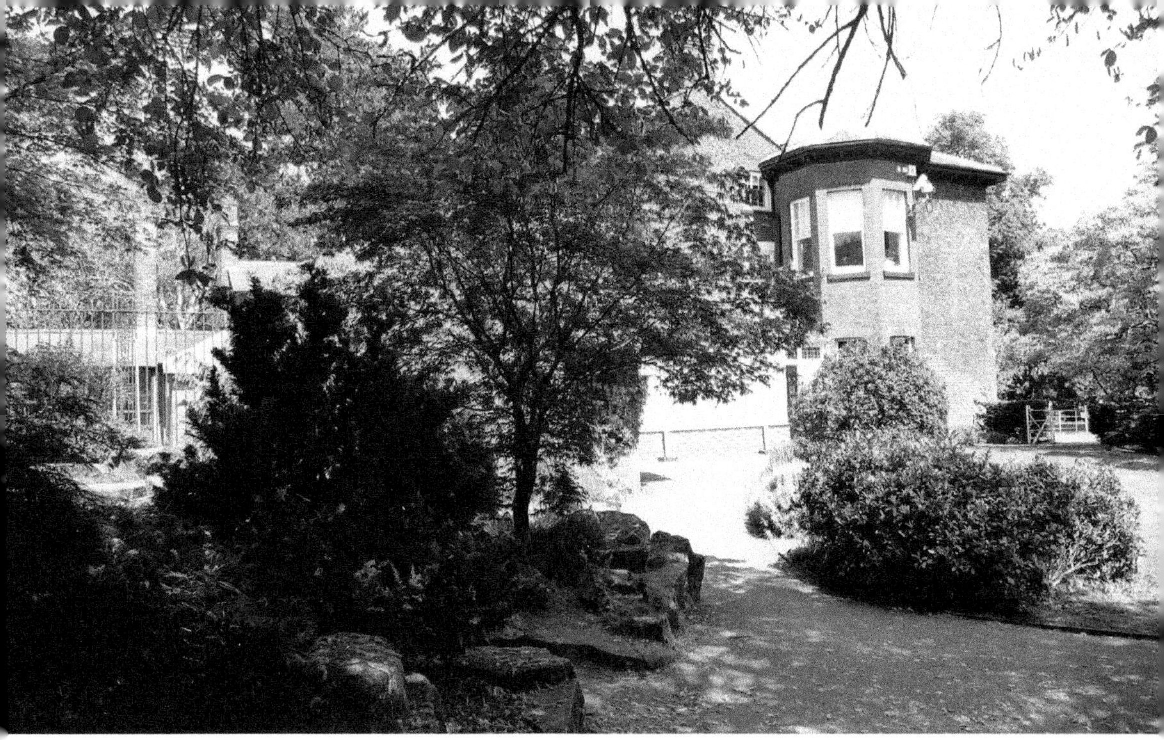

Bantock House Gardens.

them. In 1998 the council restored the gardens to Alderman Bantock's original designs, such as the rose garden and the sunken Dutch Garden. In the park there are football pitches, a small golf course, putting green and children's play areas.

Address: Finchfield Road, Wolverhampton, WV3 9LQ. Website: www.bantockhouse.co.uk.

32. Molineux, Home of Wolverhampton Wanderers

Molineux takes its name from the surname of the family that owned and lived here in the eighteenth century, and has been the home of Wolverhampton Wanderers since 1889. In 1744 Benjamin Molineux purchased a tract of land near the centre of Wolverhampton for £700 on which he built Molineux House. The building has since been a hotel (Molineux Hotel) and is now the home of Wolverhampton City Archives. In 1860 Molineux House and land were sold to Mr O. M. McGregor, who converted the estate into a hotel and pleasure park, with attractions such as a skating rink, boating lake with a fountain, croquet lawns, flower beds, walkways and lawns. The grounds were also used to stage cycle racing, athletics and football matches. Northampton Brewery purchased the land in 1889 and rented it to Wolverhampton Wanderers.

Wolves' first Football League game at Molineux was on Saturday 7 September 1889 in a 2-0 win over Notts County. It was the first purpose-built stadium built for a Football League club. It was also one of the first football grounds in Britain to have floodlights installed, which was in 1953, when the inaugural match was versus South Africa, Wolves beating the tourists 3-1. All this is commemorated in my book *Wolves Against The World – European Nights 1953–1980.*

Since those far-off days the stadium and the club have gone through the ringer on more than one occasion. Happily things now seem to be on the rise with Wolves in the top half of the Premier League, and having once again qualified for a European competition. Molineux is a great, atmospheric place to watch football.

Address: Wolverhampton Wanderers, Molineux Stadium, Waterloo Road, Wolverhampton, WV1 4QR. Website: www.wolves.co.uk.

Archives address: Wolverhampton City Archives, Molineux Hotel Building, Whitmore Hill, WV1 1SF. Tel: 01902 552480. Website: www.wolverhamptonart.org.uk/wolverhampton-city-archives.

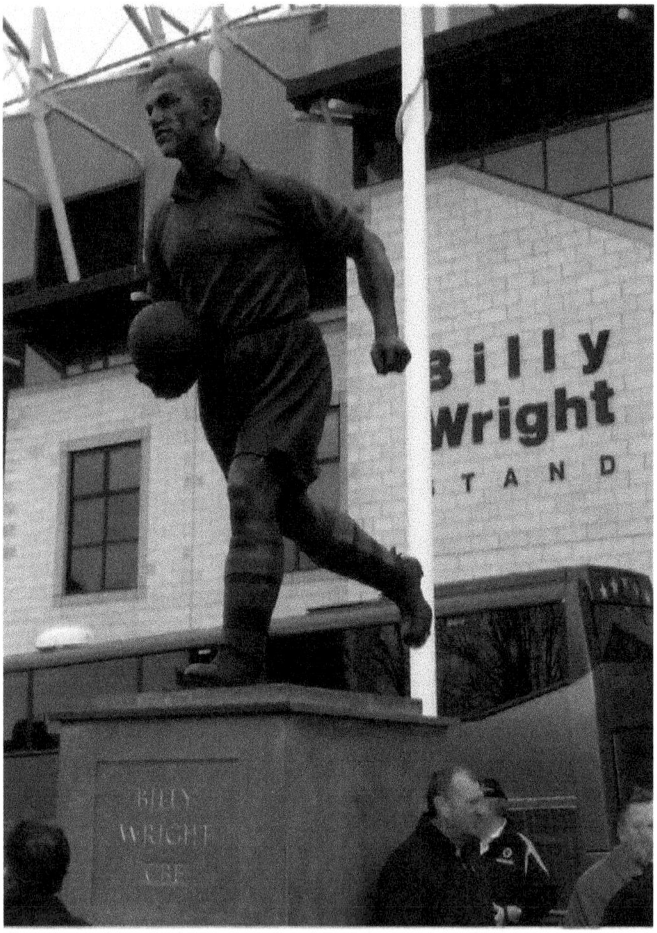

Statue of Billy Wright, Molineux Stadium, Wolverhampton.

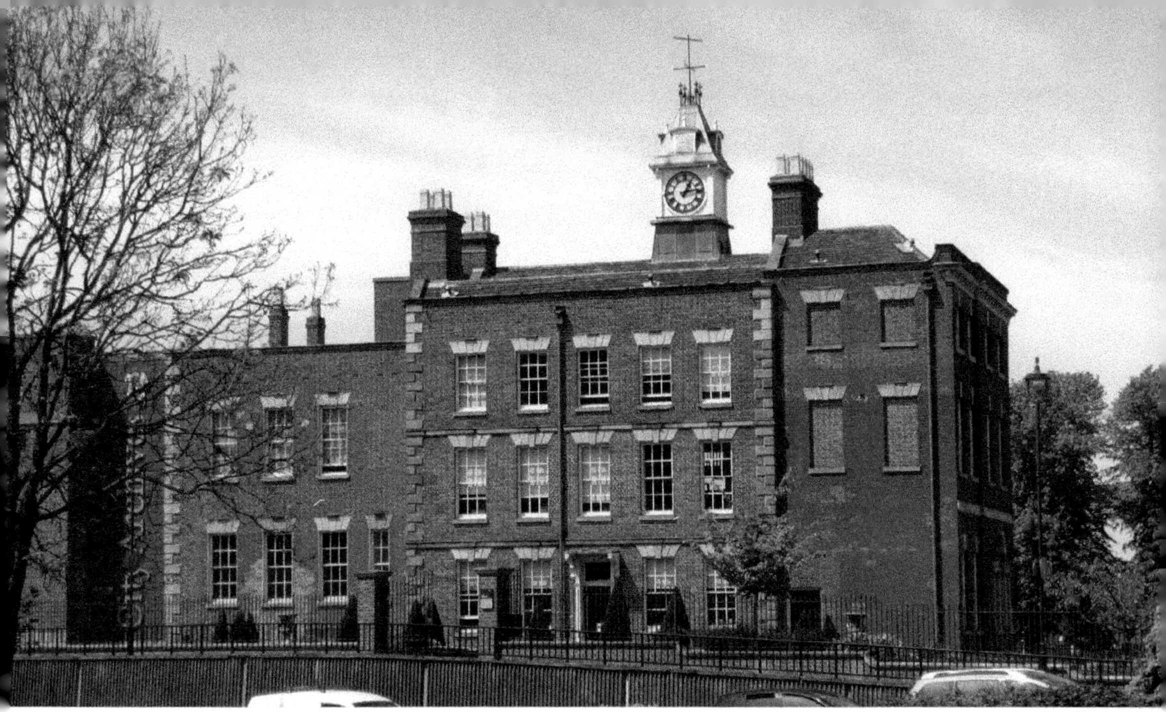

Molineux House, Wolverhampton.

33. Moseley Old Hall, Wolverhampton, and the Monarch's Way

Anyone familiar with the history of the English Civil War and the story of Charles II's escape after the ill-fated Battle of Worcester will be familiar with the part played by Moseley Old Hall in Fordhouses near Wolverhampton. The hall has been a National Trust property since 1962 when ownership was transferred by the Wiggin family.

In 1583 Henry Pitt of Bushby, a merchant, purchased the estate from the Cordsall family, building a house in *c.* 1600 on the site of an earlier building that had burnt down. The house was then known as Mr Pitt's New Hall, and later Moseley Old Hall, distinguishing it from the nearby manor house, Moseley Hall, seat of the Moseley family. Following Pitt's death in 1602 his daughter Alice, a Catholic widow, inherited the estate. She married Thomas Whitgreave in 1606. Thomas the elder died in 1626, and the estate was inherited by their son, also Thomas, a Royalist officer who fought and was wounded at the Battle of Naseby.

It was at Moseley Old Hall that Charles II took refuge in 1651. The full story follows in the next item: the Monarch's Way.

Today Moseley Old Hall is a prized visitor attraction with furniture from the Stuart period, including the original four-poster bed that Charles II slept in. The priest holes where Catholics were hidden can be viewed including the one Charles

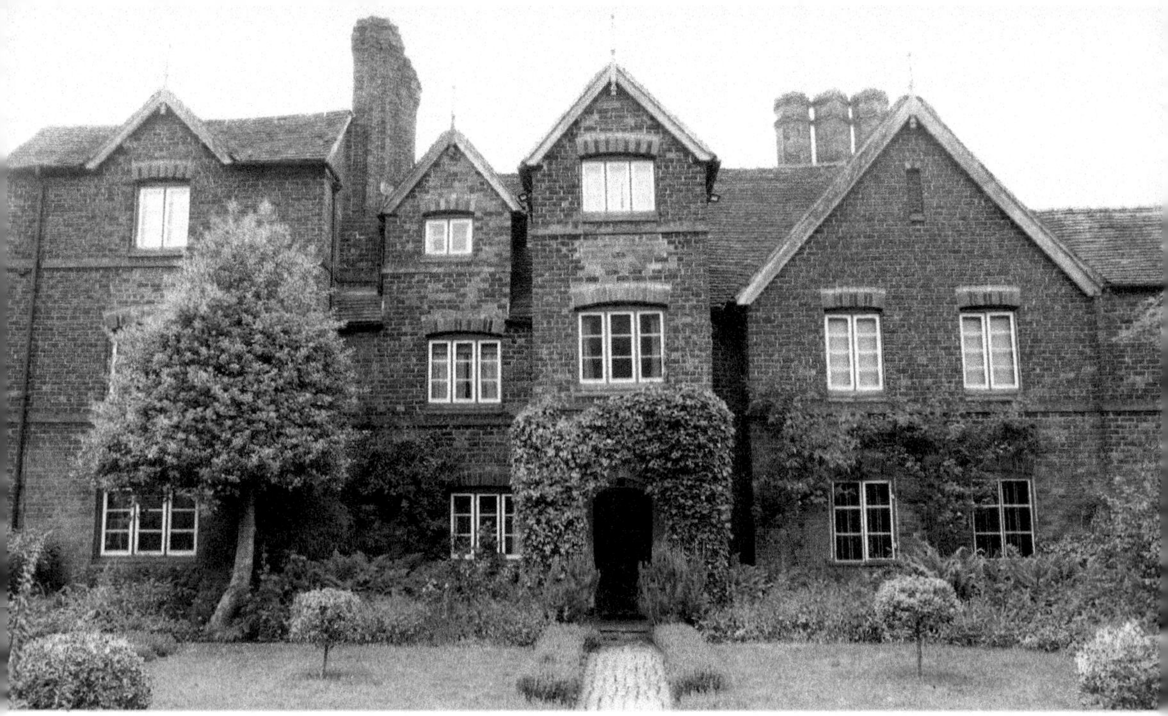

Moseley Old Hall.

hid in. Although the house is relatively small, it has marvellously evocative rooms to experience along with the informative tales told by the guides. The original half-timbered structure has long since been encased in brown brick.

Outside there is an orchard, a knot garden, topiary and a walled garden to see. Full details on the National Trust website.

Address: Moseley Old Hall Lane, Featherstone, Wolverhampton, WV10 7HY.

The Monarch's Way is a national route that plots the escape of Charles II, much of it zig-zagging across the Black Country and adjoining counties.

Following defeat at the Battle of Worcester on 3 September 1651, Charles Stuart (later Charles II) escaped the city and fled northwards in company with Lord Derby, Lord Wilmot, Charles Gifford, and a party of other loyal Royalists hoping to evade capture by Oliver Cromwell's Roundheads (no doubt remembering what they had done to his father, Charles I). Legend has it that Charles dodged out of the back door of his headquarters in the Cornmarket, near St Martin's Gate, as Roundhead soldiers entered through the front. Charles had been crowned King of Scotland at Scone Abbey on 1 January 1651 and supported by the Scots was persuaded to invade England in an attempt to regain his crown, crossing the border into England on 8 August.

The escapees stopped at the King's Arms in Ombersley for refreshments, then rode to Hartlebury where Charles parted company with Lord Derby and most of his followers. The king, together with Lord Wilmot and Charles Gifford, made for White Ladies Priory in Shropshire via Hagley, Pedmore, Whittington Manor House, where more refreshments were reputedly taken, and Wordsley, intending to try to get to South Wales and there to take ship for France. Lord Derby and his party were captured at Kidderminster and executed. Parliament put a bounty of £1,000 on Charles' head, together with a notice that whoever gave him assistance would be killed in a horrible manner.

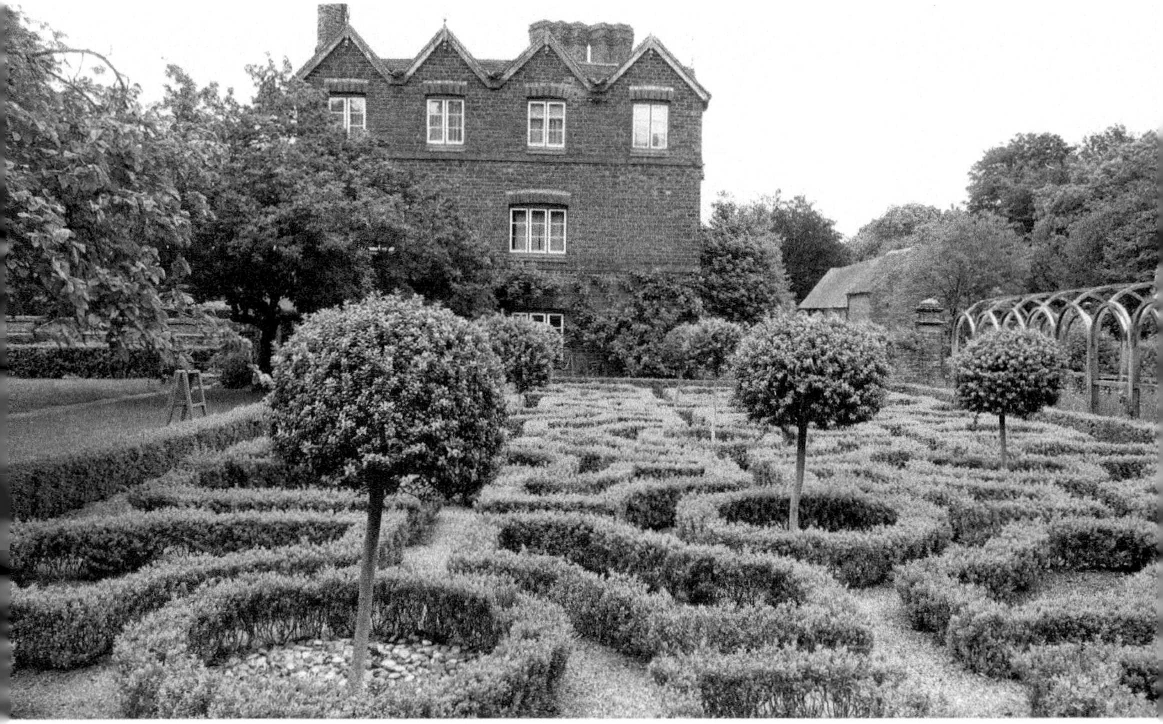

The Elizabethan Knot Garden, Moseley Old Hall.

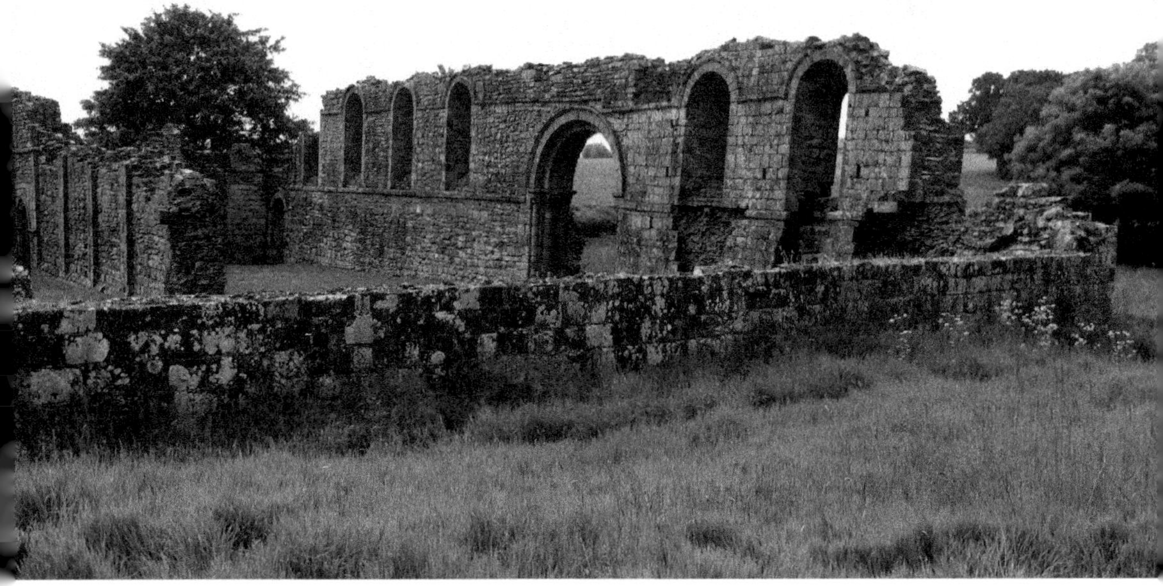

The ruins of Whiteladies Priory.

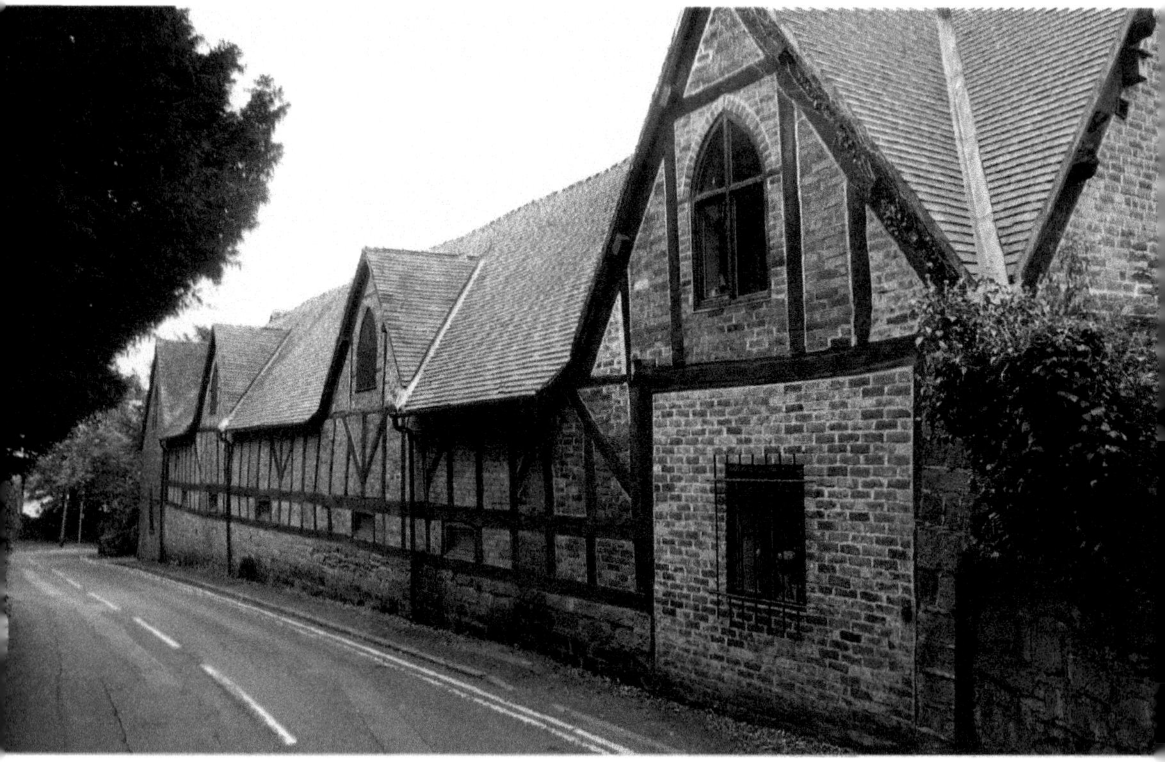

King's Barn, Madeley.

The king's party finally arrived at White Ladies Priory, a large timber-framed house built on the site of a medieval nunnery owned by the Gifford family, early on Thursday 4 September. He was cared for by Gifford's tenants, the sympathetic Penderel family, who disguised Charles as a woodsman, cutting his hair in the process. Charles Stuart was 6 feet 2 inches tall with a swarthy complexion, and no shoes could be found to fit the large royal feet, so it was necessary to slit the largest shoes that could be found in order to make them fit.

Richard Penderel led Charles to Spring Coppice near Coven Heath, where they hid, evading a company of Roundheads who had ransacked Boscobel House looking for the fugitives. Charles himself later recalled this event: 'In this wood I stayed all day without a meal or drink and by good fortune it rained all the time which hindered them, as I believe, from coming into the wood to search for men that might have fled there.'

Under cover of darkness Charles was taken to Hobball Grange, near Tong, home of one of the five Penderel brothers, and from there to Evelith Mill, near Kemberton, where they were forced to flee after they were challenged by the miller. The king was then taken to Upper House in Madeley, the home of another staunch Catholic with Royalist sympathies, Francis Wolfe, sheltering in the barn as it was deemed too dangerous to remain in the house. The barn is known today as 'King Charles' Barn'. Wolfe and Penderel scouted out the nearby River Severn crossings, but found them too well guarded by Parliamentary troops.

Next morning, 6 September, Penderel and Charles were forced to retrace their steps, this time making for another of the Gifford family's properties, Boscobel House, where they encountered another Royalist officer who had fought at Worcester, Colonel William Carless of Brewood. Charles and Carless spent all day hiding in a pollarded oak tree in Boscobel Wood. From their vantage point the pair could see Roundhead patrols searching the area. When it was deemed safe enough Charles slept for a while in Carless' arms before spending that night in one of Boscobel's priest holes.

From Boscobel the fugitives were taken by the five Penderel brothers to Moseley Old Hall, near Wolverhampton, being forced to halt at Pendeford Old Mill, when the old horse Charles was riding was unable to continue. Two of the Penderel brothers continued on with Charles, in company with Francis Yates, arriving that evening at Moseley, where Thomas Whitgreave's Catholic priest, Father John Huddlestone, bathed the king's bleeding feet.

Charles stayed two days at Moseley, hiding when required in the priest hole there (anyone visiting the Old Hall today can view the priest hole, and realise how uncomfortable hiding there must have been). On 10 September, Parliamentary troops arrived and questioned Whitgreave, who persuaded them there was nothing suspicious there. The soldiers left without searching the house.

After that close call the king was taken to Bentley Hall, near Walsall, home of Colonel John Lane and his sister, Jane Lane, who they learned was in possession of a permit for herself and a servant to travel to Somerset to visit a pregnant friend, Mrs George Norton of Abbot's Leigh. Seeing an opportunity to get to Bristol, Charles agreed to pose as Jane Lane's servant.

When word came that no ships would be sailing from Bristol to France for a month Charles continued on to the home of the Wyndham family in the village of Trent on the border with Dorset.

Boscobel House.

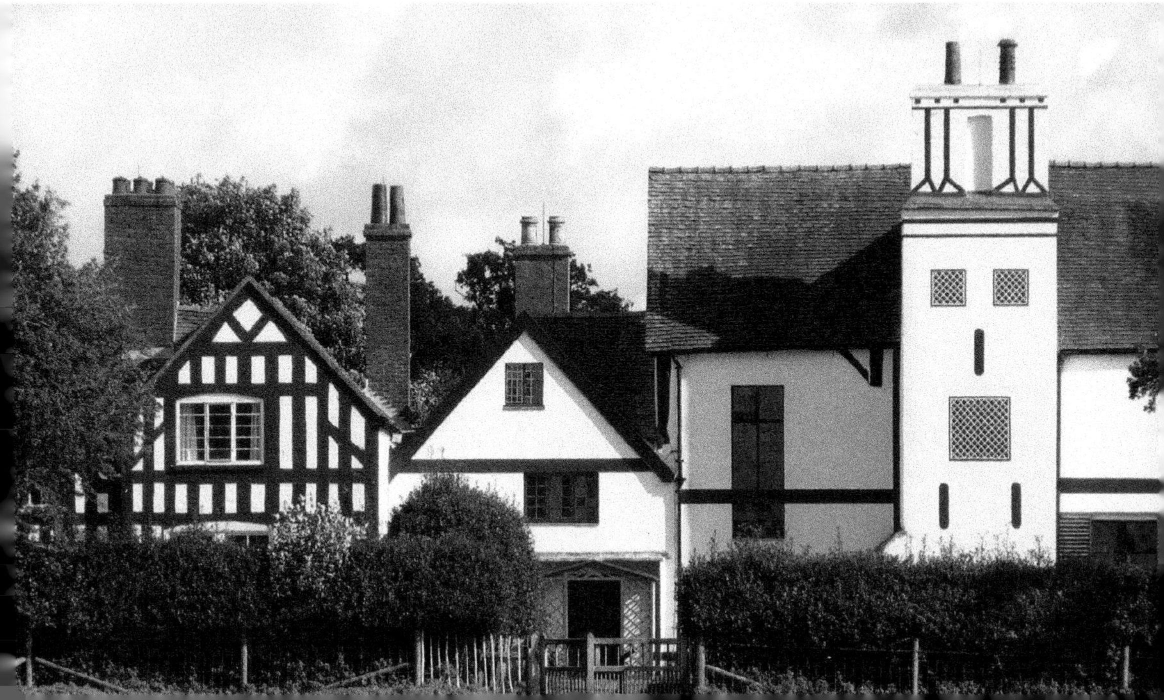

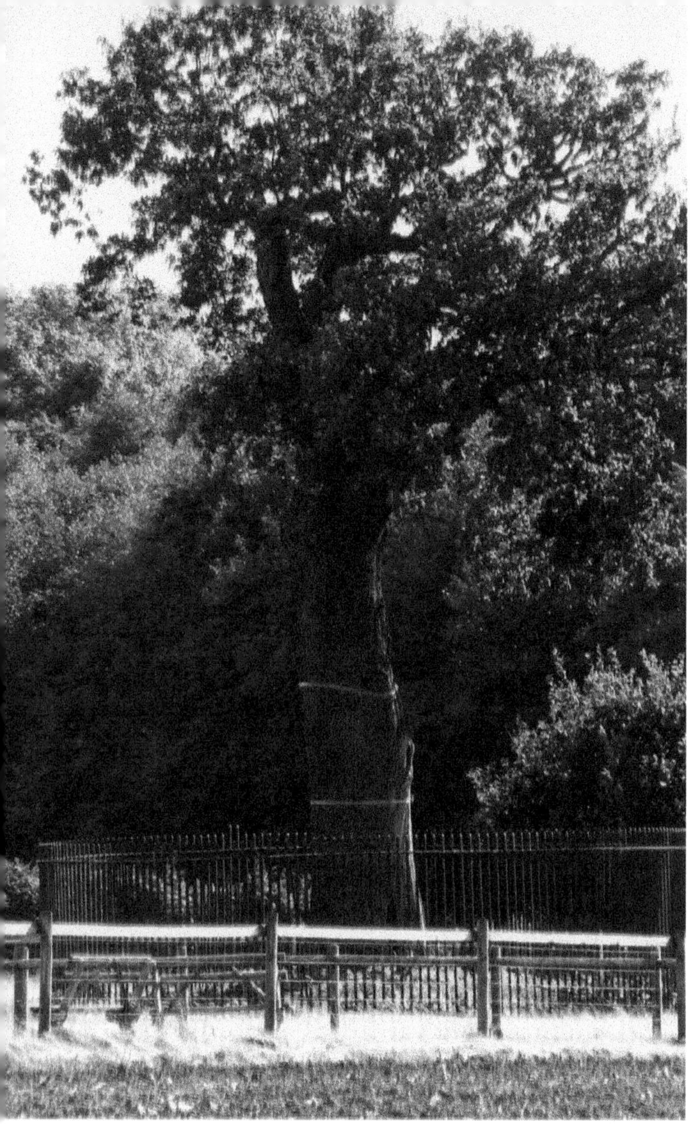

The royal oak tree, Boscobel.

Despite many setbacks and narrow escapes along the south coast, Charles finally made a successful break for freedom. He and Lord Wilmot took ship, *Surprise* (a coal boat), at a cost of £80 plus a later demand of £200 danger money, from Shoreham, near Brighthelmstone (Brighton) in Sussex to Fecamp, near Le Havre in France, landing on 16 October.

Charles Stuart spent the next nine years there until the restoration of the monarchy in 1660, following the death of Oliver Cromwell in 1658 and two years of political confusion.

The Monarch's Way is a well-marked 625-mile footpath that traces the king's escape route from Worcester to Shoreham. The annual Royal Escape Yacht Race from Brighton to Fecamp commemorates Charles' escape.

The famous episode of the Boscobel oak inspired the oak-apple day celebrations, and the name of numerous pubs: The Royal Oak. The original oak tree was so decimated by souvenir hunters that by 1712 it had been all but destroyed. The current royal oak was reputedly grown from an acorn from the original tree, which was severely damaged in a storm in 2000.

34. Northycote Farm and Country Park

Northycote Farm (Northicote) and Country Park is a delightful day out. This model working farm is operated by Wolverhampton Council, set in 90 acres of parkland. The restored Tudor farmhouse, built around 1600, with later additions and restored in the 1980s, is a real half-timbered gem. Unfortunately not open to general visitors, however it will now be used for afternoon tea by the participants in the Alpaca Walks run in association with Shareshill Alpacas. Check by emailing bec@shareshill-alpacas.co.uk.

The farm has various animals to see, plus a sensory garden and a herb garden, and of course there are lovely woodland walks, the babbling Berry Brook, and a quaint tearoom. Parking and toilets are available and admission is free. Opening times: Monday to Sunday 9 a.m. to 4 p.m., and tearoom Tuesday to Sunday 10 a.m. to 3 p.m. Northycote is not far from Moseley Old Hall, and there is a walk between the two to be enjoyed (details on the National Trust Moseley Old Hall website).

Address: Underhill Lane, Bushbury, Wolverhampton, WV10 7JF. Tel: 01902 397906. Tearoom tel: 01902 784200.

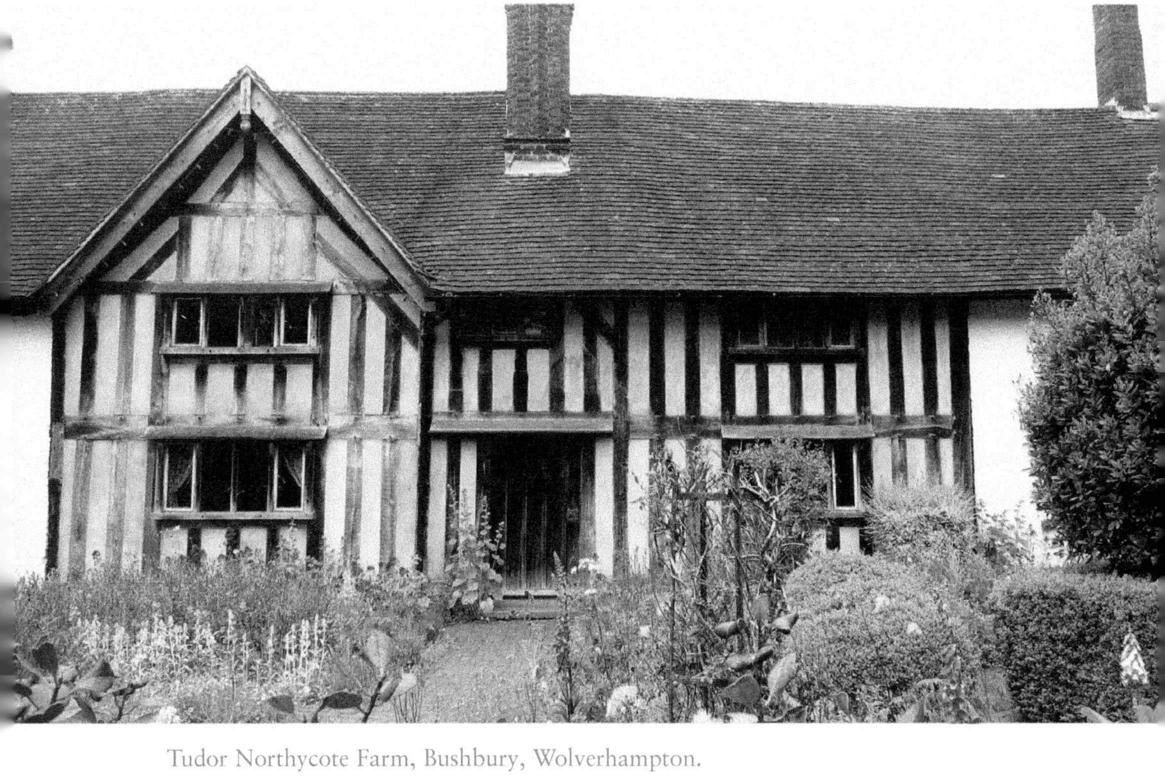

Tudor Northycote Farm, Bushbury, Wolverhampton.

35. Wightwick Manor, Compton

The Grade I listed Wightwick Manor in Compton is one of my favourite places. One of the finest examples of the Arts and Crafts movement, it is packed out with fabulous artefacts.

The building of Wightwick (pronounced Wittik) Manor began in 1887 when Samuel Theodore Mander purchased the Wightwick Manor estate and employed renowned Liverpool architect Edward Ould to design a new and spectacular home. The old Tudor manor house was repaired and the new manor built in two phases in the Tudor half-timbered venacular style, with jettied storeys, gabled roofscapes, barley-twist chimneys, skeleton herringbone and wishbone timberwork, and trefoiled and quatrefoil cusps. The manor is a magnificent mock-sixteenth-century delight.

For everyone marvelling at the beauty of the exterior upon entering the interior through the lovely entrance door their enjoyment is heightened by the wonderful sights that greet their eyes. Everywhere is beauty. The fabulous furniture and tapestries, pastels, sketches and paintings. Pre-Raphaelite works of art by such artists as Dante Gabriel Rossetti, Evelyn De Morgan, Ford Madox Brown, Lucy Madox

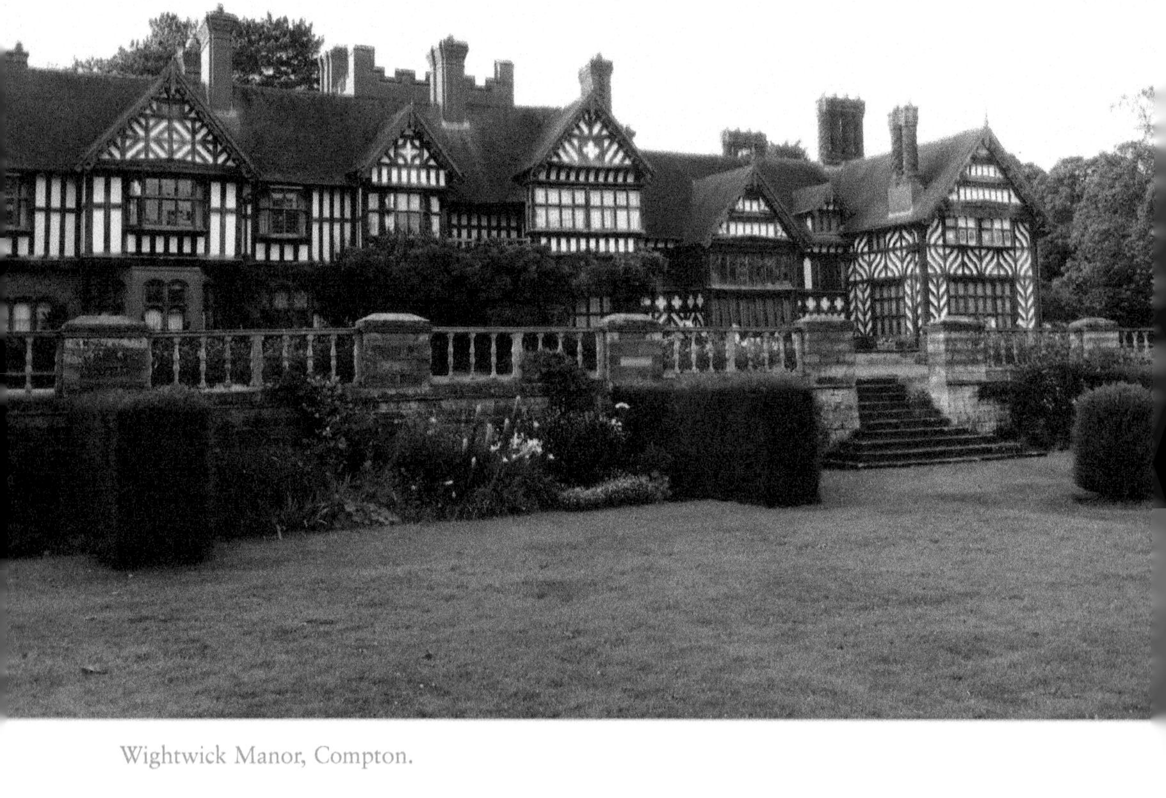

Wightwick Manor, Compton.

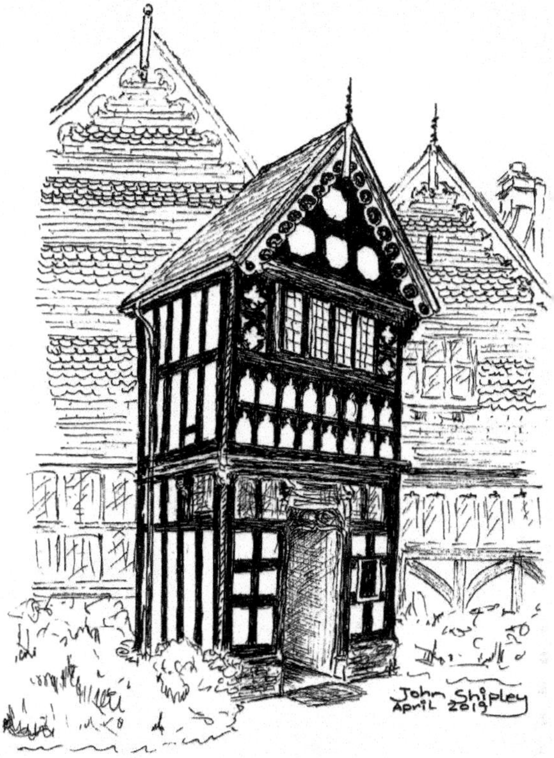

Main entrance of Wightwick Manor, Compton. (Pen and ink drawing by John Shipley)

Brown, Marie Spartali Stillman, May Morris, Edward Burne-Jones, William Holman Hunt, John Everett Millais and Elizabeth (Lizzie) Siddal. Wonderful William Morris wallpapers and fabrics are everywhere to be seen, along with Charles Kempe glass and plaster reliefs, and William De Morgan tiles.

The National Trust took over the property in 1937, when Geoffrey Mander and his second wife Rosalie gave it to the charity, the couple becoming live-in curators. The 17-acre gardens were laid out by T. H. Mawson. Check out the opening times on the National Trust website, and make sure to visit the tearooms and gallery.

Address: Bridgnorth Road, Wightwick Bank, Compton, Wolverhampton, WV6 8EE.

36. Wolverhampton's Twenty-one Locks

This amazing flight of twenty-one locks on the Birmingham Mainline Canal Network is a sight worth seeing. Terminating at Aldersley Junction where the canal meets the Staffordshire and Worcestershire Canal, the flight begins at Broad Street Junction in the city centre, with a total water level fall of 121 feet (37 metres) spread over 2 miles. Built by James Brindley, the full 22.5-mile (36-km) route from Birmingham opened in 1772.

The 21 Lock Trail (brochure available) is around 1.75 miles (2.8 km) long.

37. Sedgley Beacon Tower

Situated on Beacon Hill in the midst of the Beacon housing estate, just outside Sedgley town centre, at 778 feet (237 metres) above sea level, is the Grade II listed Sedgley Beacon Tower, dating from around 1846. It was built either by Lord John Wrottesley, 2nd Baron Wrottesley, an acclaimed amateur Victorian astronomer, or a local quarry/landowner by the name of Mr Petit, either as a folly or on behalf of Lord Wrottesley. The crenellated tower is 50 feet (15 metres) tall by 7 feet (2 metres) in diameter, built using Gornal sandstone. The tower is often fondly referred to locally as the 'Monument' or the 'Big Whistle'. There has been a beacon on the hill for over 400 years, with some form of tower existing prior to 1700. From the top it was claimed that on a clear day it was possible to see the Bristol Channel.

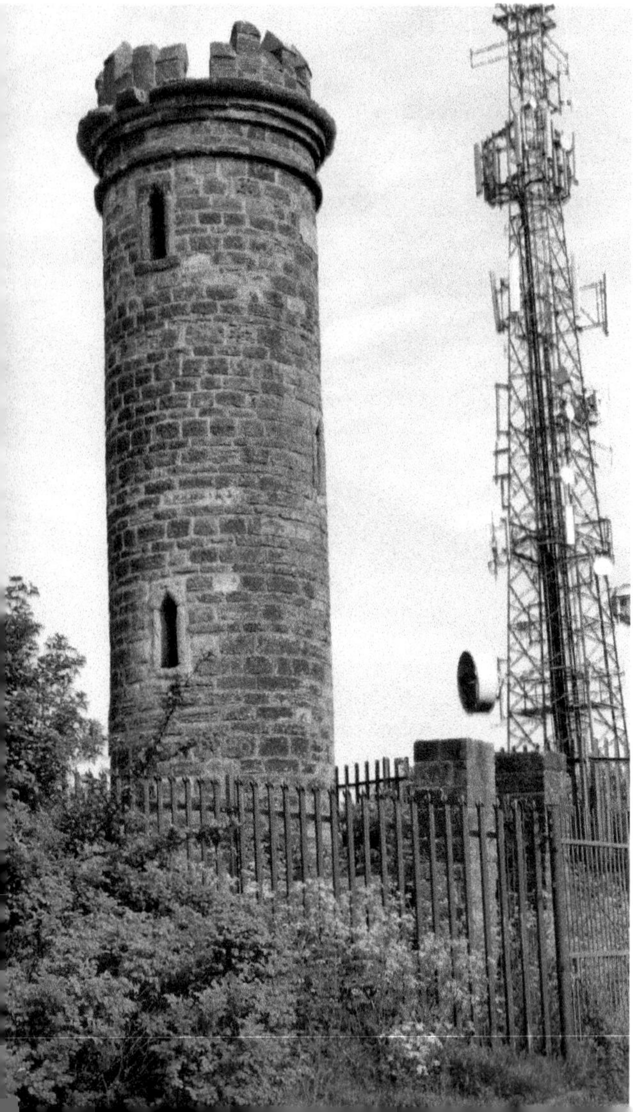

Sedgley Beacon Tower.

Sadly the tower is currently in a state of disrepair; parts of it are crumbling and as such has had to be fenced off. The bottom 8-foot section of the internal spiral staircase is now longer there, removed by the local council to prevent accidents. Fallen masonry litters the ground around the tower. The local Tenants and Residents Association have been working hard to raise sufficient funds and National Lottery grants to restore the tower to its former glory.

An intrinsic part of the chain of beacons in England to signal warnings of impending invasions, the beacon would have been lit in August 1588 to warn of the arrival of the Spanish Armada. The signal flame would have been visible from Cannock Chase and Barr Beacon. Beacon fires have since been lit to mark special occasions, such as in 1887 to mark the Golden Jubilee of Queen Victoria, and more recently to mark the Silver and Golden Jubilees of Elizabeth II.

Local legend suggests druids once used the hill as a place to practise their faith. The hill was also used by Yorkist soldiers during the Wars of the Roses and by Roundhead Colonel Sir William Brereton and his Parliamentary troops during the siege of Dudley Castle.

A Site of Importance for Nature Conservation, Beacon Hill is a spot well loved by local and visitors alike for its walks and views, and was the scene of intensive limestone quarrying (brown or black lime) from possibly earlier than the seventeenth century until the early twentieth century, which has left topographical features such as ridges and gullies from the excavations and spoil heaps that once scarred the landscape. The hill is part of the 5-mile (8-km) 'Limestone Walk' that also includes Wren's Nest, Hurst Hill and Dudley Castle Hill. Leaflets are available from Dudley Council.

Address: Beacon Hill, Beacon Lane, Dudley, DY3 1NA.

38. St Wulfruna's Cross, St Peter's Collegiate Church, Wolverhampton

Standing in St Peter's Garden near the south door of the old church is a 13-foot 6-inch- (4.1-metre-) tall blackened sandstone pillar, or column. A cylindrical Saxon preaching cross, with a gradual taper towards the top, the shaft of which is mounted on a 7-foot 10-inch- (2.4-metre-) diameter base with four rounded steps. This is St Wulfruna's Cross, also known as the Wolverhampton Cross and the St Peter's Garden Cross. Once thought to date from around AD 850, but now believed to be late tenth century, possibly AD 994. There is a counter belief that the cross has Roman origins and was brought to its present site in the mid-ninth or late tenth century from the Roman city of Viroconium (modern day Wroxeter, Shropshire) or from Wall. Saxon stone masons added carvings on the slightly tapering sides. The

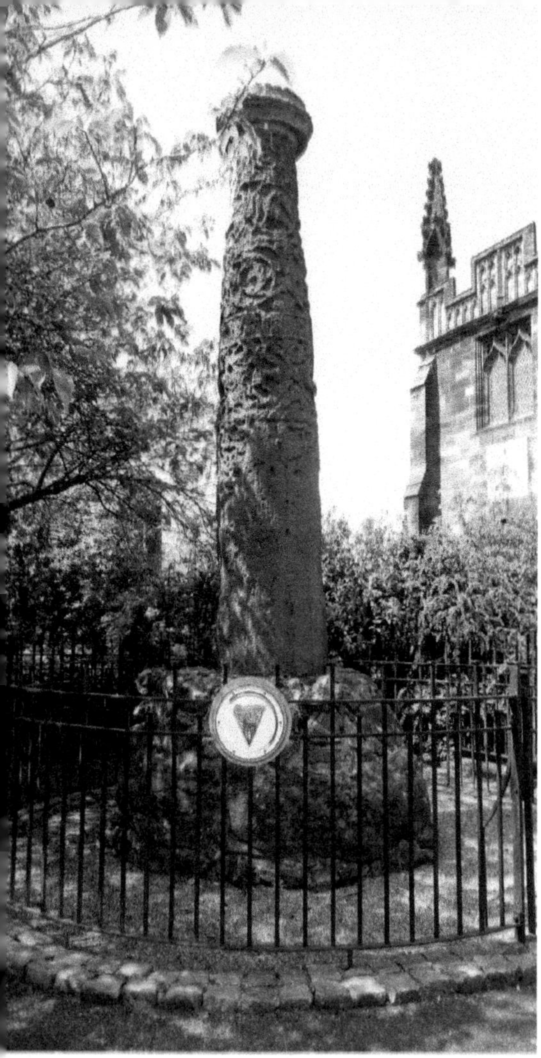

Left: St Wulfruna's Cross.

Below: St Peter's Collegiate Church, Wolverhampton.

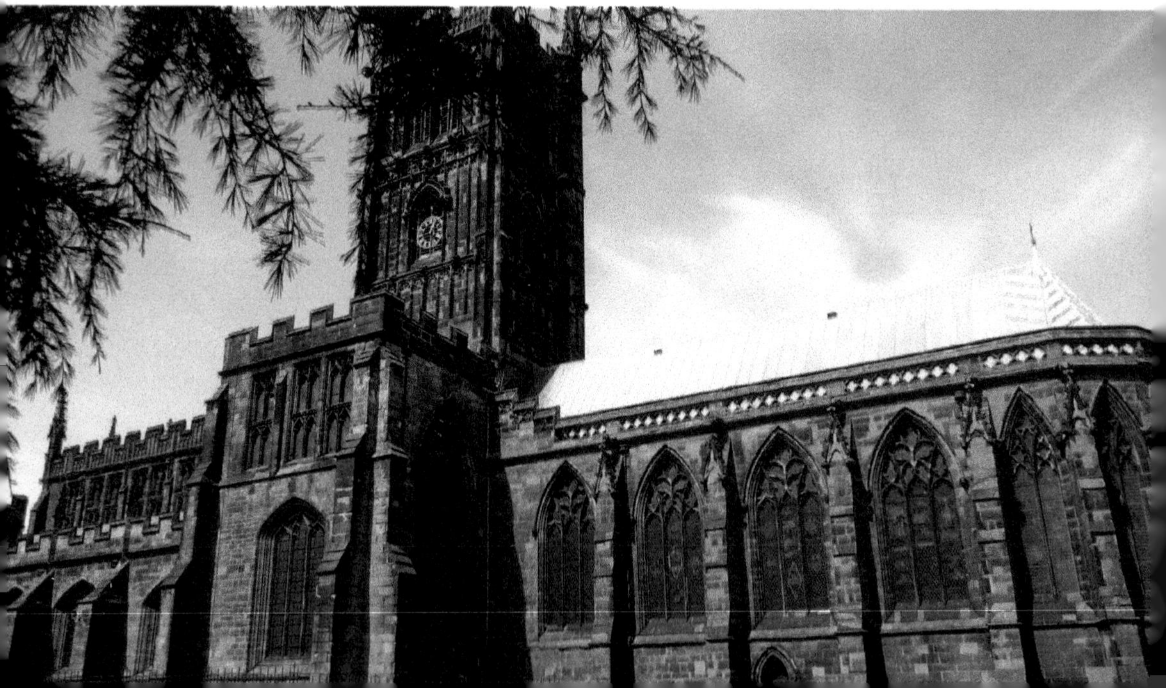

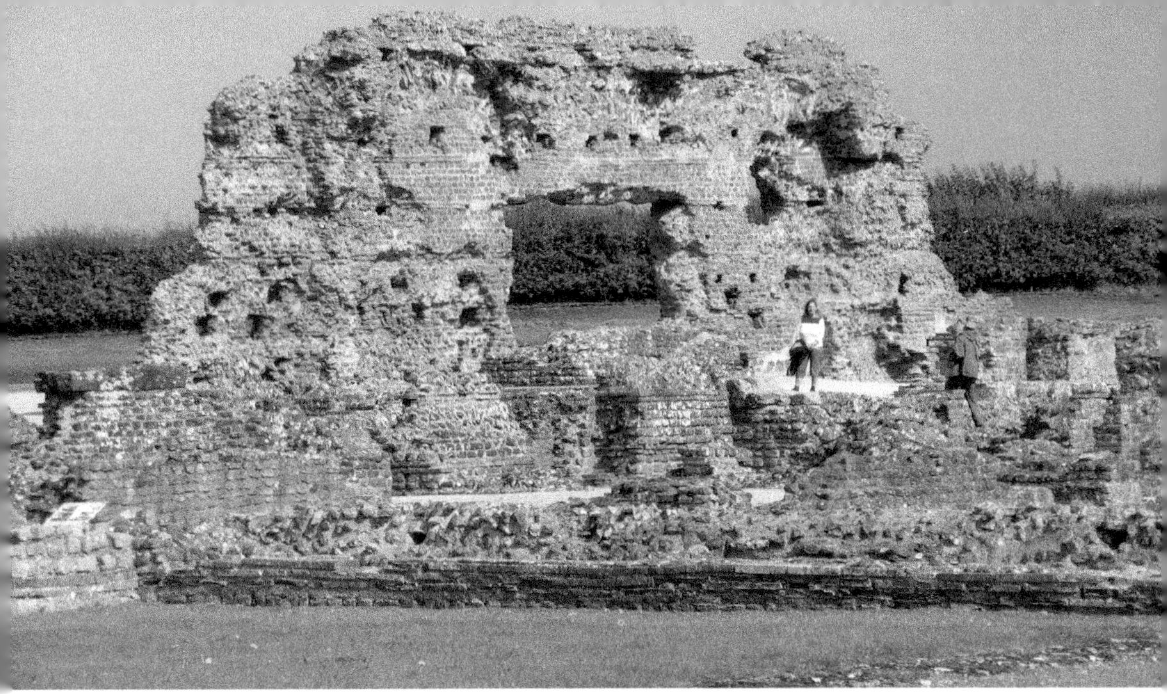

Above: The Old Work, Viroconium, (Wroxeter).

Right: Stone tablet commemorating Wulfruna's endowment of the Monastery of St Mary's at Hamtun in AD 994.

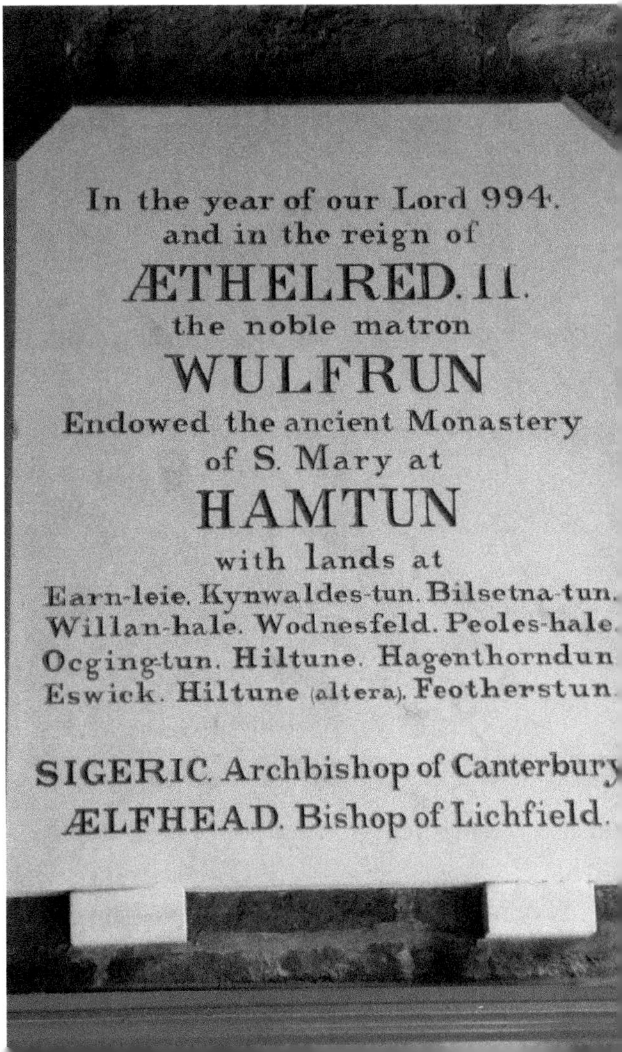

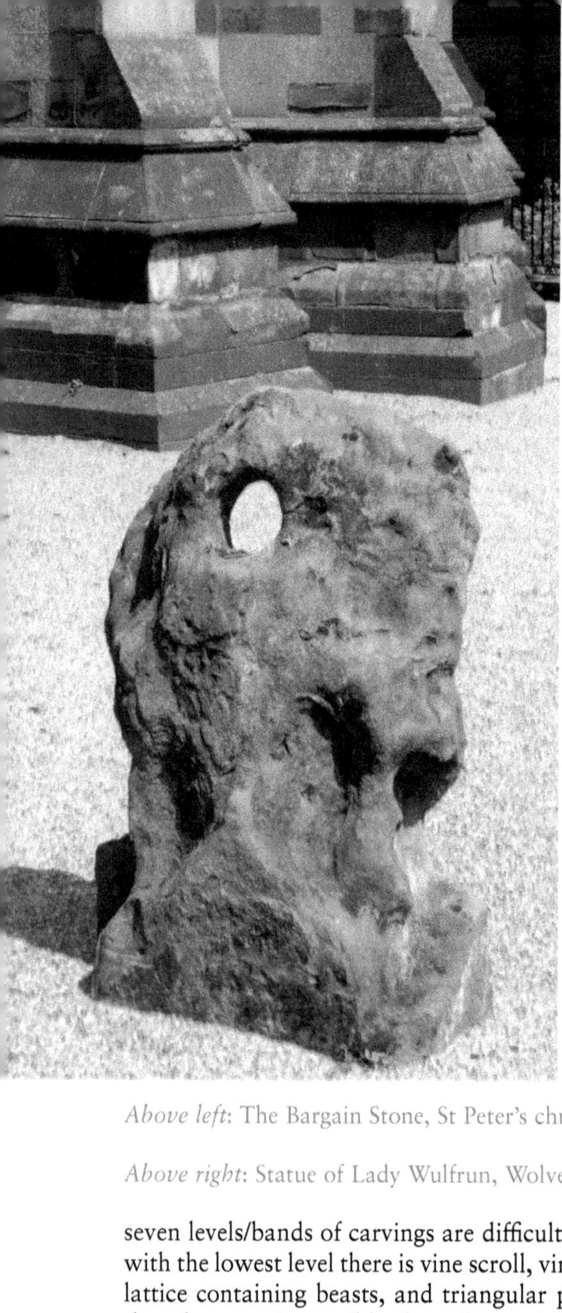

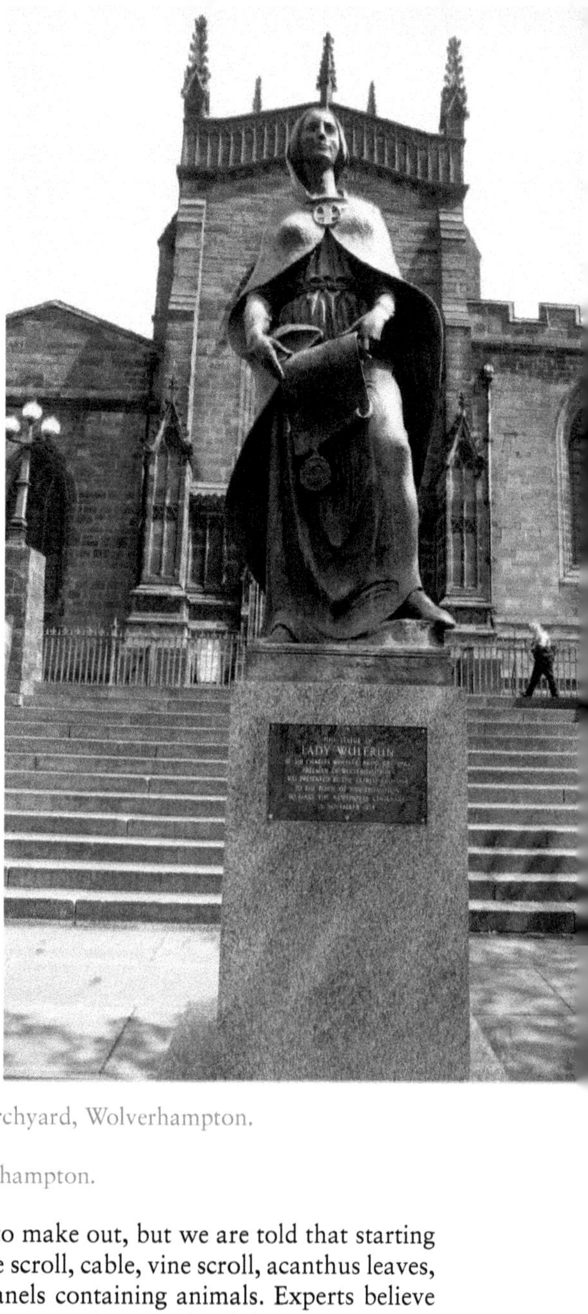

Above left: The Bargain Stone, St Peter's churchyard, Wolverhampton.

Above right: Statue of Lady Wulfrun, Wolverhampton.

seven levels/bands of carvings are difficult to make out, but we are told that starting with the lowest level there is vine scroll, vine scroll, cable, vine scroll, acanthus leaves, lattice containing beasts, and triangular panels containing animals. Experts believe that the cross is possibly the only surviving example in England that demonstrates the southern continental baroque style of the mid-ninth century. There is a plaster cast of the cross in the Victoria and Albert Museum in London. Tradition has it that in around AD 659 King Wulfhere of Mercia founded the Abbey of St Mary where St Peter's stands today; however, the suggested existence of this or of a Saxon monastery on this site has yet to be proven.

St Peter's Collegiate Church is a Grade I listed structure built in the fifteenth century, of red sandstone and in the Perpendicular style. In the Domesday Book the church is listed as being dedicated to St Mary, which changed to St Peter's in the mid-twelfth century. There seems little doubt that the present church was constructed on an earlier Anglo-Saxon religious site that certainly existed in 994. A stone tablet in the porch of the church commemorates Wulfruna's endowment of the monastery of St Mary at Hamtun in 994, calling her the noble matron. The church was for centuries a Chapel Royal, and from 1480 it was a Royal Peculiar.

Near the church is the 'Bargain Stone'. Some say this is a rare example of a holed standing stone, which was used for the practice of shaking hands through the hole to seal a bargain. Others suggest that it may just be a fallen gargoyle stone from the roof.

Lady Wulfruna was the wife of Earl Athelme, of Mercia, mother of St Wulfric of Burton, and was the supposed granddaughter of Æthelred I. Legend has it that in AD 948 she was kidnapped by Viking King Olaf, and was imprisoned at Tamworth, from where she later escaped. Wulfruna died and was buried in either 996 or 1005.

At the top end of Gorsebrook Road in Wolverhampton is Lady Wulfruna's Well, constructed here in 1901 and restored in 1980. Legend has it that the original well was situated near St Peter's Church.

39. Lady Godiva's Cross, St Bartholemew's Church, Upper Penn

Standing on a hill overlooking Penn Common is St Bartholemew's Church. In its graveyard on the south side of the church are the remains of an Anglo-Saxon preaching cross, dating from around 1050, known as Lady Godiva's Cross. There are also the remains of a medieval cross, this is on the west side of the church. Both crosses were discovered in 1912. The base and stem of the earlier cross has part of its round shaft, atop a base, mounted on three steps. The medieval cross also has three steps, plus a socket stone and a shaft, and in the 1900s a carved head was added. It is possible that this cross was originally on top of Lady Godiva's Cross. Penn is possibly an Anglo-Saxon settlement, although there may have been a Celtic settlement there before that period. The Domesday Book states that Lower Penn was owned by Lady Godiva of Merica. Upper Penn (also known as Penn Under) was owned by her son, Lord Algar (which means 'Elf Spear'). Godiva is the Latin form of the Anglo-Saxon Godgift (gift of God). She is best remembered for her legendary naked ride through Coventry. She was married to Earl Leofric, one of the most powerful men in the kingdom. Lady Godiva died 10 September 1067 at Evesham and is buried in Evesham Abbey.

The original church on the site was built by Hugh de Bushbury in around 1200 and was dedicated to St John the Baptist, later changing to St Bartholemew. In 1765 the tower was encased in brick. The north arcade of the church dates from the fourteenth century and the west part of the church and tower date from the fifteenth century.

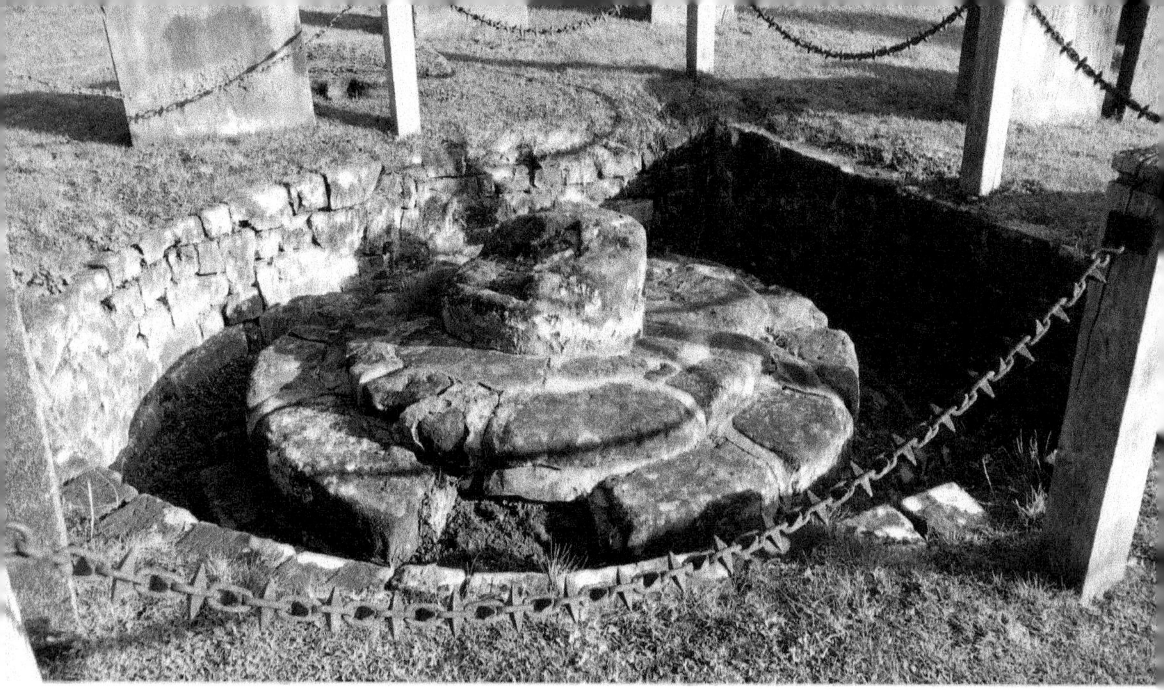

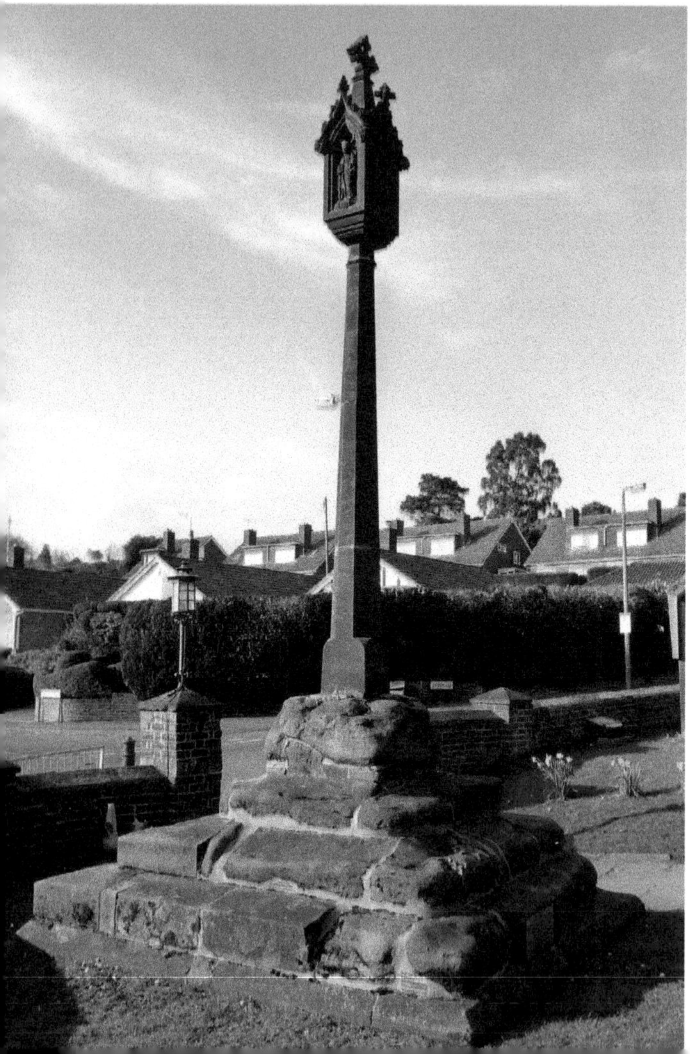

Above: Lady Godiva's Cross, Upper Penn.

Left: Medieval cross, St Bartholemew's churchyard, Upper Penn.

The area of open land below the church is known as Penn Common, which was once dotted with numerous small farmsteads, a place where families used to go, and still do, for good walks and picnics – watch out for flying golf balls.

Address: St Bartholemew's Church, No. 57 Church Hill, Penn, Wolverhampton, WV4 5JB. Tel: 01902 576809. Website: www.stbarts.org.uk.

40. The Grand Theatre, Wolverhampton

This delightful Grade II listed building is one of the finest theatres in the country. The theatre first opened on 10 December 1894, designed by architect Charles J. Phipps and built by local builder Henry Gough at a cost of around £10,000. The 123-foot-long façade is virtually unchanged since its opening, when the debut performance was *Utopia Limited* by the celebrated D'Oyly Carte Opera Company,

Wolverhampton's Grand Theatre.

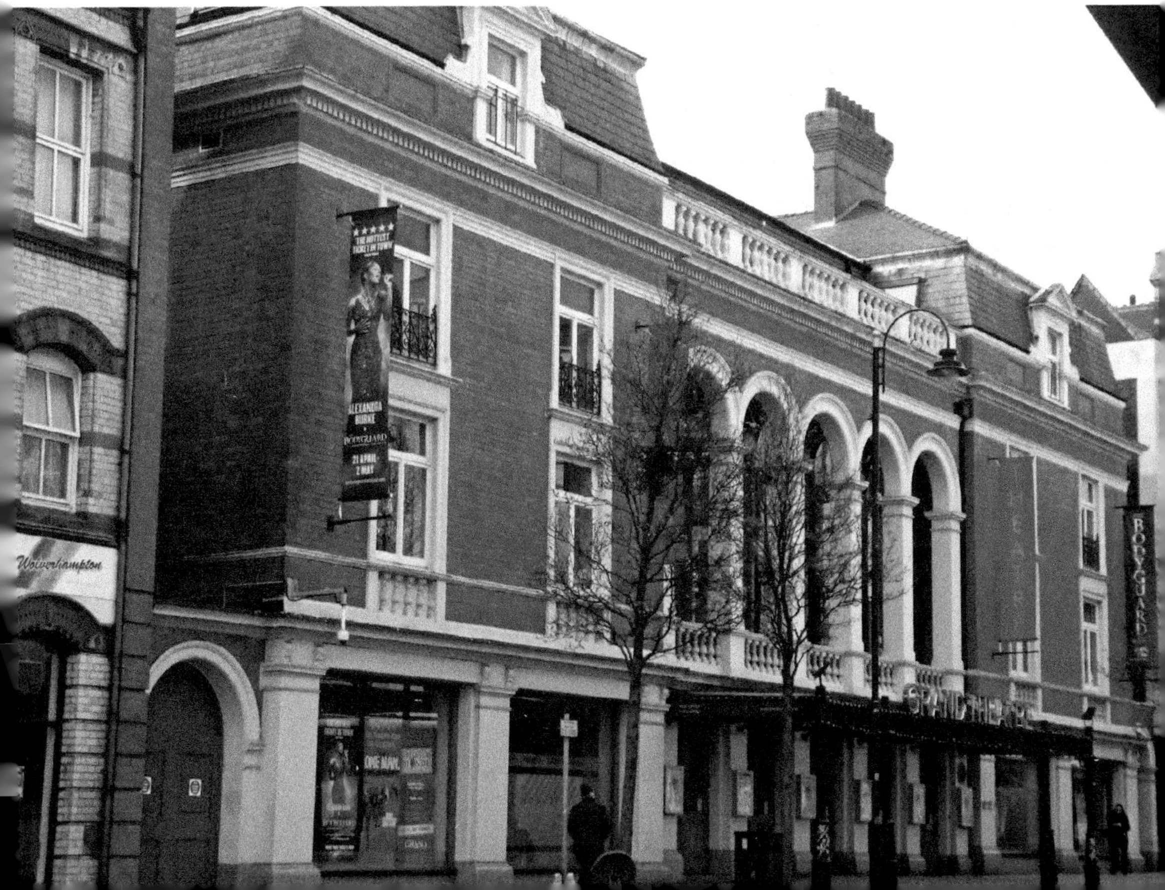

played to a capacity audience of 2,151, which was class segregated: gentry in the Dress Circle, middle-class folks in the Stalls, and working folks in the Gallery/Upper Circle, known as the sixpenny gallery, where tickets could not be pre-booked (they had to be queued for). Huge numbers of famous people have trodden the boards at the Grand: Charlie Chaplin, Winston Churchill – suffragettes threw stink bombs at him and tore up seats – Lloyd George and Marlene Dietrich, just to name a few. Declining audience numbers in the late 1950s and a fire were no doubt factors in the Myatt family's decision to sell the theatre to the Local Authority for £74,000. The theatre was renovated in 1973, and almost closed for good in the 1980s when 'Save The Grand' was launched, the theatre reopening 31 August 1983. The latest refurbishment saw the theatre reopen its doors in 2017.

Address: Wolverhampton Grand Theatre (1982) Ltd, Lichfield Street, Wolverhampton, WV1 1DE. Tel: 01902 429212. Website: www.grandtheatre.co.uk.

The Walsall Metropolitan Borough Area

41. Barr Beacon

One of the highest points in the area is Barr Beacon with its 60-acre (25-ha) Local Nature Reserve where in historic times beacon fires were lit to warn of approaching invaders, such as to warn of the Spanish Armada in 1588. In these more peaceful times beacon fires are lit more in celebration. It was fired up for Queen Elizabeth II's Coronation, and her Silver, Golden and Diamond Jubilees.

The hill is 774 feet (236 metres) above sea level, and until 1918 was owned by the Scott family of Great Barr Hall, later being auctioned off. The winning bid was made by Colonel J. H. Wilkinson, who transferred ownership to a trust, which in 1972 was transferred to Walsall Council, who now manage the site for the Barr Beacon Trust. The trust had opened the site to the public in 1919.

Historic finds on the hill include a Neolithic mace head and Neolithic or Bronze Age stone hammers, plus Roman coins.

On the summit there is a war memorial dating from 1933 and a reservoir. Passing across the hill is the Beacon Way, a 25-mile (40-km) long-distance walking trail through Staffordshire and the West Midlands, taking its name from Barr Beacon. The trail begins at Sandwell Valley Country Park, extending to Gentleshaw Common, north of Burntwood, Staffs, where it joins with the Heart of England Way.

Traditional claims are that from the summit it's possible to see eleven counties: West Midlands (obviously), Staffordshire, Shropshire, Warwickshire, Worcestershire, Herefordshire, Gloucestershire, Leicestershire, Northamptonshire, Oxfordshire and Powys in Wales.

Barr Beacon has been designated a 'Dark Sky Discovery Site' so it's a good spot to do a bit of stargazing (check out the Walsall Looks Up website).

Other nearby lowland heaths are Pelsall North Common, Brownhills Common and Shire Oak Park.

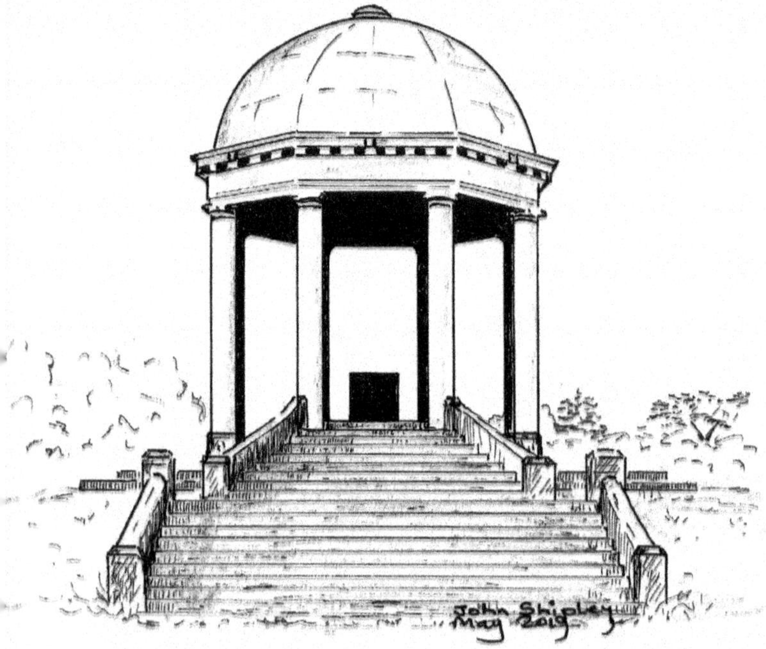

Barr Beacon War Memorial. (Pen and ink drawing by John Shipley)

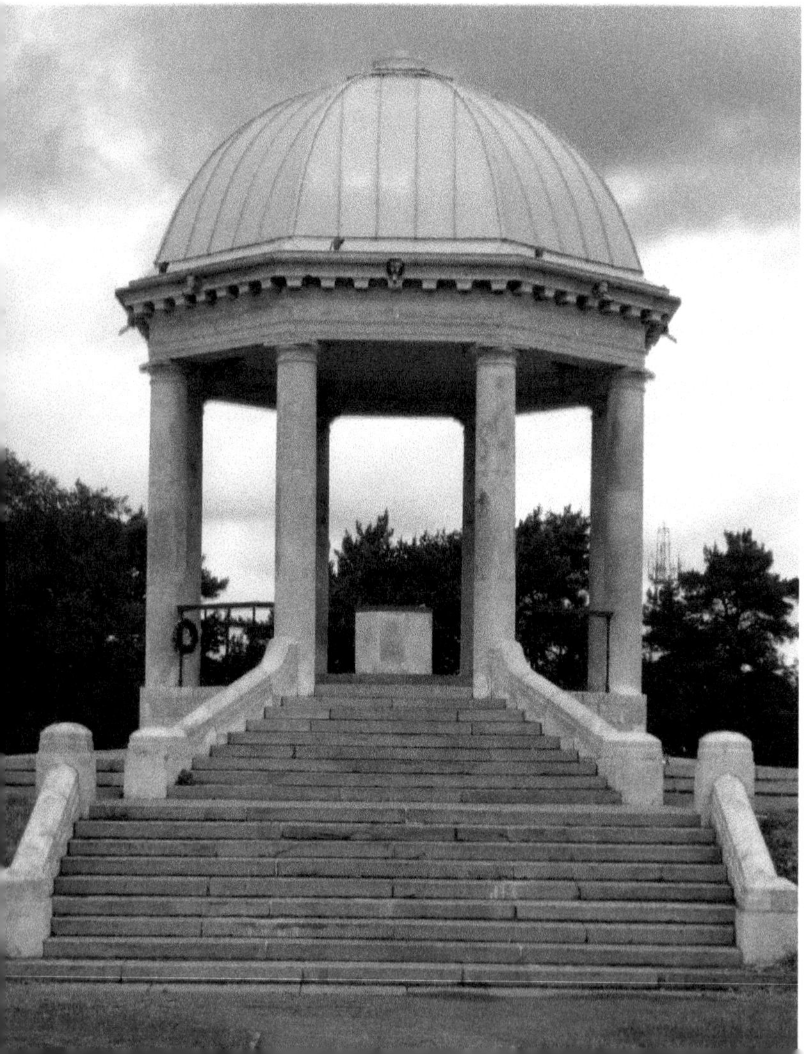

Barr Beacon War Memorial.

42. Moorcroft Wood Local Nature Reserve, Moxley

Moorcroft Wood Nature Reserve in Moxley was created on an abandoned industrial site that was mostly previously covered by Moorcroft Old Colliery and blast furnaces. Walsall Council claim that this is 'a bostin place for bats' where several species have been spotted including the water bat known as Daubenton's Bat. The sunken areas on the reserve were created by collapsed mine workings. The underlying rocks on the site have been dated to the Carboniferous period around 300 or so million years ago. In 1904 all industrial activity on the site ceased, mainly because the unstable nature of the terrain made it susceptible to fire and flooding. Before then raw materials were mined for use by the Moorcroft Ironworks in the production of pig iron for blast furnaces. Also, the abundance of surface quarried glacial clay and sand facilitated the establishment of a brickworks on the site. Although there is no definitive evidence, it is thought that mining may possibly have been carried out here during Roman times.

In 1904 the site was purchased by the Wednesbury Hospital Board to help with patient's from Moxley Isolation Hospital convalescence. The hospital closed in 1995.

The reserve is owned and managed by Walsall Council. Entrance is free, but there are no toilets or other facilities. Warden guided tours are available from Monday to Friday, 9 a.m. to 5 p.m. Call 01922 654220 for more details. Address: Hawkswood Drive, Moxley, Walsall, WS10 7BW.

43. Great Barr Hall and Park

The Grade II listed Great Barr Hall is today nothing more than a decaying ruin, and features on the Buildings at Risk register. The hall, then known as Nether House, was acquired in the mid-seventeenth century by Richard Scott. Around 1777 Joseph Scott, later Sir Joseph Scott, 1st Baronet Scott of Great Barr, replaced the old house with a two-storey, nine-bay mansion, built in the Strawberry Hill Gothic Revival style. The hall was extended a number of times in the late 1800s. Prior to that in around 1788 the house was leased to Birmingham Quaker gunmaker Samuel John Galton for the family's summer residence (also see Warley Woods Abbey). Galton was a prominent member of the famous Lunar Society, who sometimes met here. The Scott family died out in 1909, and in 1911 the hall was purchased by the local hospital board and opened as St Margaret's Mental Hospital. In 1918 the grounds became a nature reserve. The hall received its Grade II listing in 1971, and was abandoned in 1978, sadly left to decay. Three of its six original lodges still survive. In the 1960s my band played a gig for the doctors and nurses at the hall.

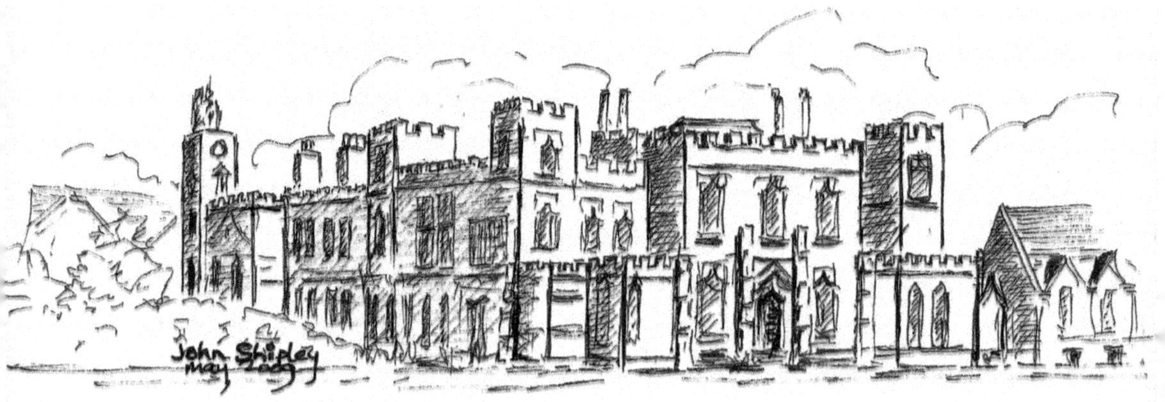

Artist's impression of Great Barr Hall. (Pen and ink drawing by John Shipley)

44. Rushall Hall

The original manor house at Rushall was built during the twelfth century, probably by the de Boweles family, who held the manor from around 1230 to 1346. That structure was replaced some time around 1400 by Geffrey Ive. One of only three known examples of medieval fortified houses in the West Midlands, the 300 feet (91 metre) × 175 feet (53 metre) rectangular area is surrounded by a 21-feet- (6.4-metre-) high crenellated curtain wall, with a notionally square two-storey fortified gatehouse built in the late fifteenth century by the Harpur family behind an earlier gate archway. A third storey was added in the late 1500s/early 1600s, but this was largely destroyed in the mid-1800s. Situated within the walls is a more modern house, largely Victorian but with some of the older walls incorporated into the structure. At one time the hall was surrounded by a moat.

During the English Civil War the hall was fortified for Parliament by Sir Edward Leigh, a lay author and Member of Parliament, and suffered two sieges. The first was in 1643 while Sir Edward was absent, leaving his wife to valiantly defend the property against the troops of Prince Rupert, who took the hall, placing Colonel Lane in command. The second was in May 1644 when, after a short siege by the forces of the Earl of Denbigh, the hall once again became a Roundhead stronghold.

Unfortunately, it is not currently possible to visit the hall as it is privately owned. Address: At the end of Leigh Road, off Mellish Road, Walsall.

Some 12 to 14 metres north-west of the hall is an earthen mound believed to be a hlaew, an Anglo-Saxon or Viking burial mound, with a 10-feet- (3-metre-) wide encircling ditch that is approximately 36 feet (11 metres) in diameter and 7 feet (2.2 metres) deep at its maximum point. Finds of fragmented human bones have been discovered along with Saxon coins. This feature is difficult to see and is currently fenced off.

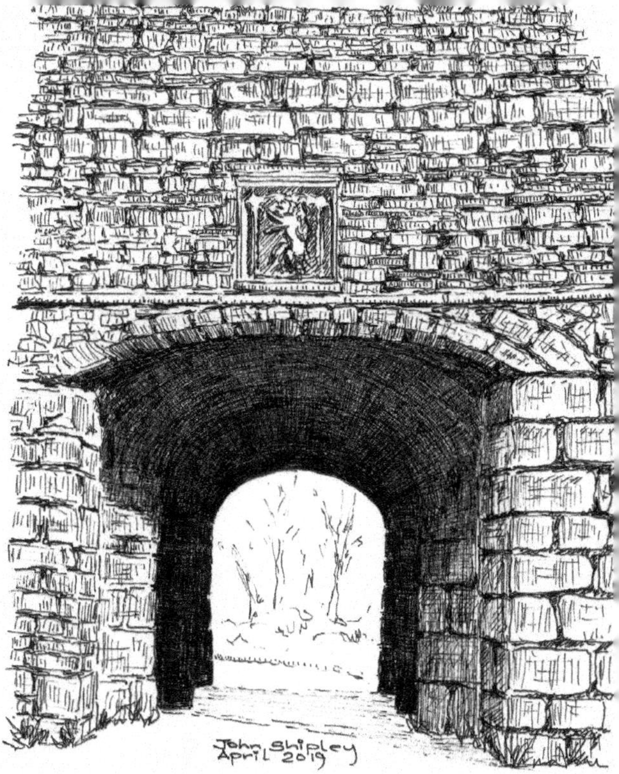

Rushall Hall gatehouse. (Pen and ink drawing by John Shipley)

Not far away are Park Lime Pits Local Nature Reserve and Park Lime Pits Country Park, a beautiful 12.45-acre (just over 5-ha) area of beech woodland, with two pools, created by the Victorians on the site of old limestone quarries. It is a wildflower haven for birds, bats and waterfowl where over 300 different species of plant have been identified. A place where limestone has been quarried since Roman times, they used it for roads such as Watling Street and for buildings such as at Wall (Letocetum). During the Industrial Revolution limestone was used as a flux for smelting iron. Mining on the site ceased around 150 years ago.

Parking can be found on Park Road off Daw End.

45. Castle Old Fort, Stonnall

Castle Old Fort in Stonnall is a slight univallate (having a single circuit of ramparts) promontory Iron Age hill fort, ovoid in shape and oriented north-east to south-east, situated near the ancient Chester Road on Castle Hill's southern side. Covering an area of around 4 acres (1.6 ha), the fort is around 560 feet (170 metres) long by 460 feet (140 metres) wide, with a ditch varying in width from around 3 to 6 feet (1 to 2 metres) and up to 13 feet (4 metres) in depth, surrounding earth ramparts varying from 3 to 6 feet (1 to 2 metres), and around 26 feet (8 metres) in height. Discoveries on the site have been a barbed flint arrowhead and an iron spearhead, plus Roman coins and pottery. The main entrance to the fort is on the north-east side. In general the earthworks are relatively well preserved, although quarrying has destroyed some of the site including what is believed to have been a second entrance to the fort. Traces of another ditch have been found, possibly indicating that at one time the fort was bivallate (a double circuit of ramparts). Part of the interior of the fort is occupied by a private dwelling – a late sixteenth-century jettied two-storey, half-timbered house that was moved from Montgomeryshire in Wales to this site in 1936. The plantation on the hill probably dates from the mid-nineteenth century. Unfortunately, at the present time the site is not open to the public, but it is possible to see some of the ramparts from Castle Hill Road.

Address: Castlebank Plantation, No. 135 Castle Hill Road, Walsall, WS9 9BD.

46. Rough Wood Country Park, Short Heath

Rough Wood Country Park in Short Heath, Willenhall, was in private ownership until the 1950s when the site was given to Willenhall Council. In 1989 it became Walsall's first nature reserve. Rough Wood, incorporating Rough Wood Chase, is one of the few remaining ancient woodlands. Altogether the site consists of six separate nature reserves. Rough Wood has a series of pools, and represents around 10 per cent of the oak woodland in the West Midlands despite much of the woodland being felled in the sixteenth century on the king's orders. Bentley Haye is a large area of wet grassland packed with aquatic insects and amphibians, such as the Great Crested Newt, which was first spotted here in 2011. Wood Farm was, as its name suggests, once a working farm that suffered from the building of the M6 Motorway, which now bisects the reserve. The Piggeries is the smallest of the sites and was once part of a farm. Sneyd Reservoir is the largest of the bodies of water on the chase. It was created originally to serve and maintain the water levels of the local canals. Oily Goughs is a strange name, deriving from a man named Gough who used to have a scrapyard here. There are three pools here.

Rough Wood Chase, adjacent to Bailey's Pool, a haven for local fishermen, includes Beechdale Park. First mention of the Chase was in the twelfth century as part of the Bentley Hay district of Cannock Forest, which was a royal hunting preserve that covered an enormous area including much of Walsall, Sutton Park and Cannock Chase. In those days it was against the law for any peasant to poach any of the plentiful wild deer and game that roamed there.

The Bentley Coal Seam runs through the site, causing the land to suffer greatly from the sinking of bell pits to mine surface coal. Examples of these depressions, caused by sinking, can still be seen. Bell pits were a primitive method of mining that were susceptible to flooding as well as sinking, so when working in them became dangerous, a new pit was started.

The reserve has walks and trails and closes at dusk.

Check out: http://cms.walsall.gov.uk/index. Car parking is at the end of Hunts Lane, WV12 5NA.

47. The White Hart, Caldmore

Now a block of flats, the White Hart at Caldmore Green in Caldmore (pronounced Karma by the locals), an area of Walsall, was once the home of Royalist George Hawe, a staunch supporter of Charles I during the English Civil War. He built the house in the second half of the seventeenth century, replacing an earlier timber-framed structure, although some of the old timber was reused. Tradition has it that Queen Henrietta spent at least one night here on her way to reinforce her husband, Charles I, at Edgehill.

In 1817 the inn was converted into a public house called Ye Olde White Hart. According to legend this house is a spooky place. During refurbishment in the 1870s the mummified arm of a child was discovered in an attic chimney. It was believed to be the arm of a hanged felon; however, subsequent pathology tests revealed that the arm was not from the 1600s, but was from more recent times. It was on display in Walsall Museum, which is sadly now closed.

During the Civil War the West Midlands was split in two in its support. The Royalists had George Hawe of Caldmore (mentioned above); Sir Thomas Leveson of Dudley Castle; Colonel Lane of Bentley Hall; William Hopkins of Oakswell Hall, Wednesbury, who was captured in 1664 at the fall of Rushall; John Persehouse of Reynold's Hall, Walsall; and Sir Thomas Holte of Aston Hall. The Parliamentarians

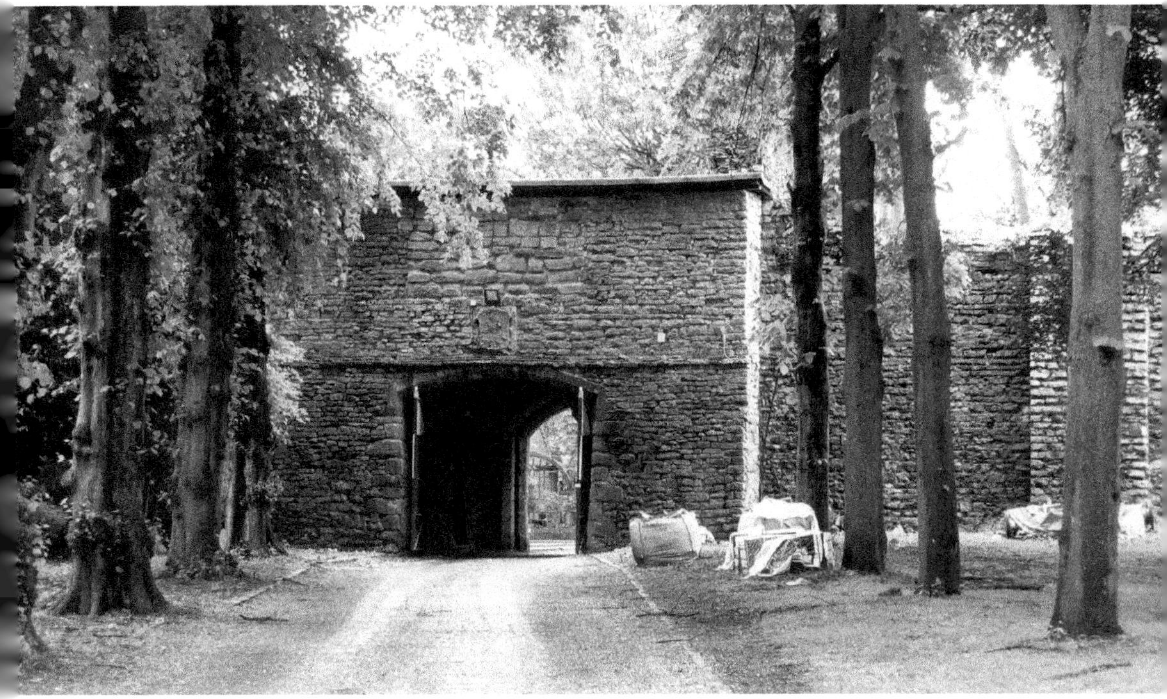

Gatehouse and wall, Rushall Hall, Walsall.

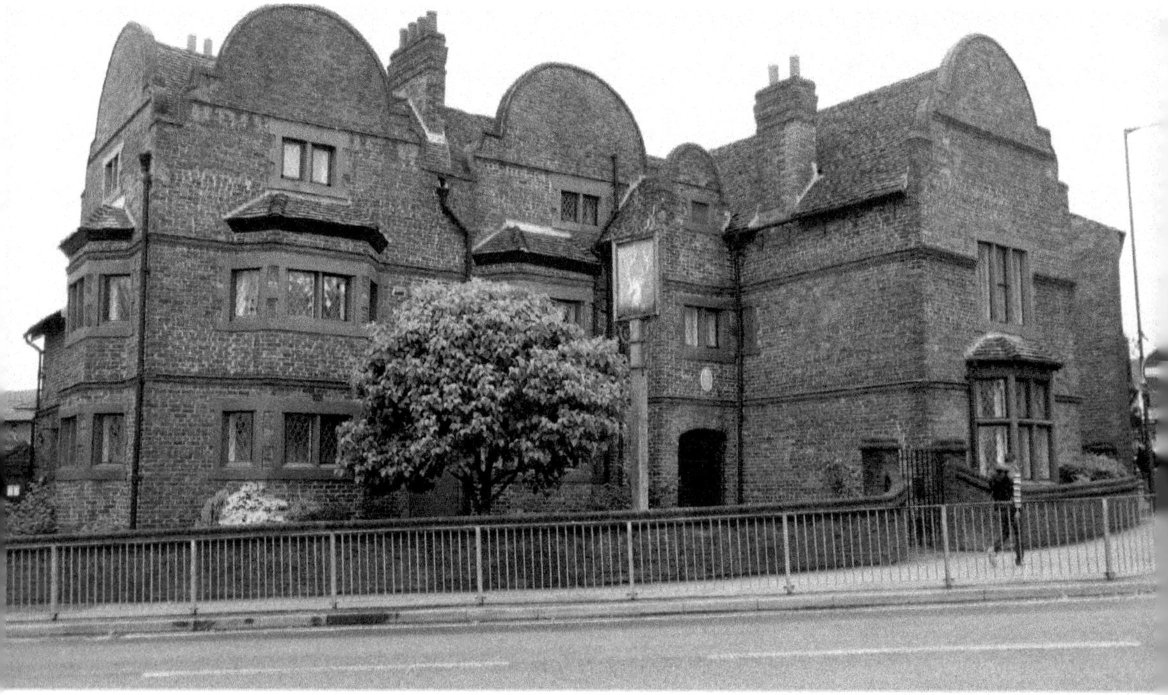

The White Hart, Caldmore, Walsall.

had Sir Richard Leigh of Rushall Hall; Edward Dudley of The Greenhouse in Tipton (roughly where Mad O'Roukes Pie Factory is today), who fought at the Battle of Tipton in 1644; Simon Montford of Bescot Hall (where Bescot Park is today); Thomas Parkes of Willingsworth Hall; Captain Henry Stone of Walsall; and Colonel 'Tinker' Fox of Walsall (commander of Edgbaston Hall), who was defeated at the Battle of Stourbridge Heath in 1644, somewhere around where Mary Stevens Park is today.

Address: Calmore Green, Walsall, WS1 3RW.

48. Shire Oak Park Nature Reserve

This 8.5-acre (3.44-ha) park in Walsall Wood is owned and managed by Walsall Council. The Shire Oak was an ancient oak tree that traditionally marked the boundary between Walsall and Shenstone. Sadly the old tree no longer exists, as it was lost in the 1890s. Shire oaks were trees of folk legend under which Anglo-Saxons would have held folkmoots or a 'thing', which were early assemblies of elders, lawmakers, etc. in Germanic society. The word 'thing' is derived from 'Þing' in which the 'Þ' is pronounced 'th'.

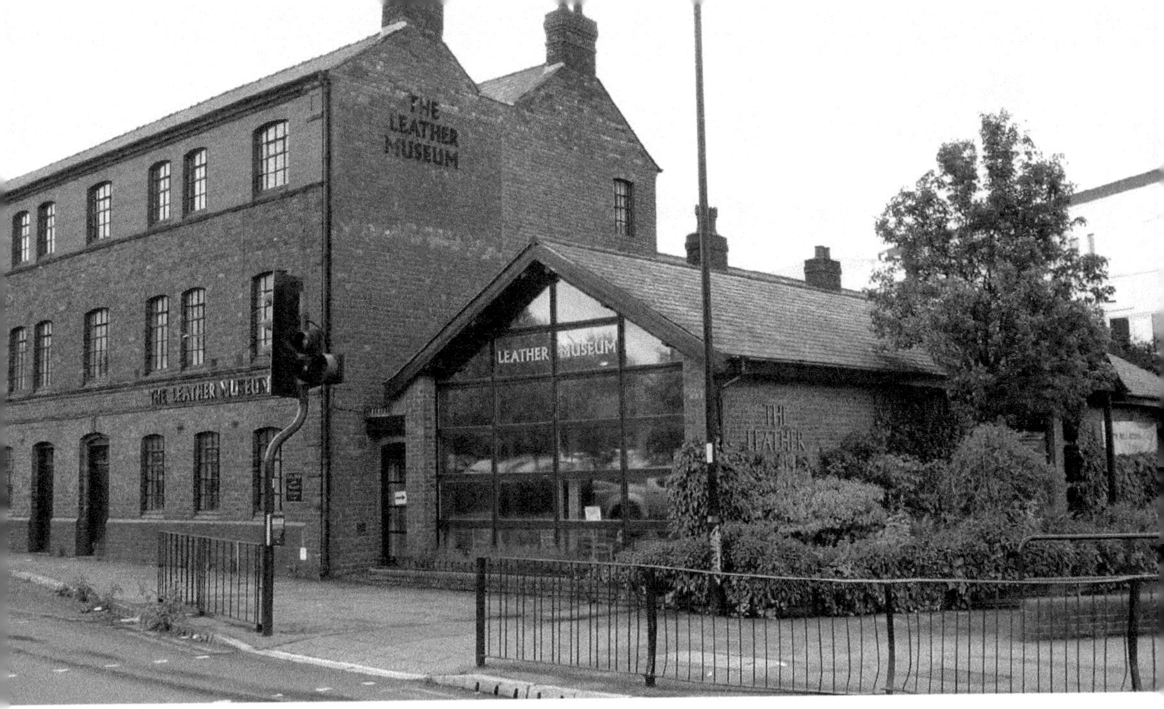

Walsall Leather Museum.

The park is a wonderland of wild meadows (wildflowers in summer), native woodlands and flowering heathland with waymarked paths to hike. There are many species of birds and amphibians to spot, and don't forget to keep an eye out for deer. From the thirteenth century the park was part of the Royal Forest of Cannock. In those days it was against the law to poach one of the king's deer. The faces of the disused sand quarry are home to mining bees and cuckoo bees.

Parking is available in Andrews Road, off Shire Ridge, which in turn is off the Lichfield Road. Admission is free.

Adjoining the southern end of the park is the site of Castle Old Fort, Stonall.

49. Walsall Leather Museum

This marvellous museum celebrates Walsall's great leather traditions of saddle making (by royal appointment), also manufacturing wallets, purses, gloves, horse bridles and accoutrements. Over ninety companies still operate in Walsall's leather trade, exporting to countries all around the world. Admission to the museum is free, which is located in a renovated old Victorian factory building, where visitors can watch demonstrations by skilled leather workers. You can also take part and make your own keyring. There is a shop, gardens and a picnic area. Guided tours are available. See website for opening times.

Address: Walsall Leather Museum, Littleton Street West, Walsall, West Midlands, WS2 8EW. Tel: 01922 652208. Website: www.go.walsall.gov.uk/leathermuseum.

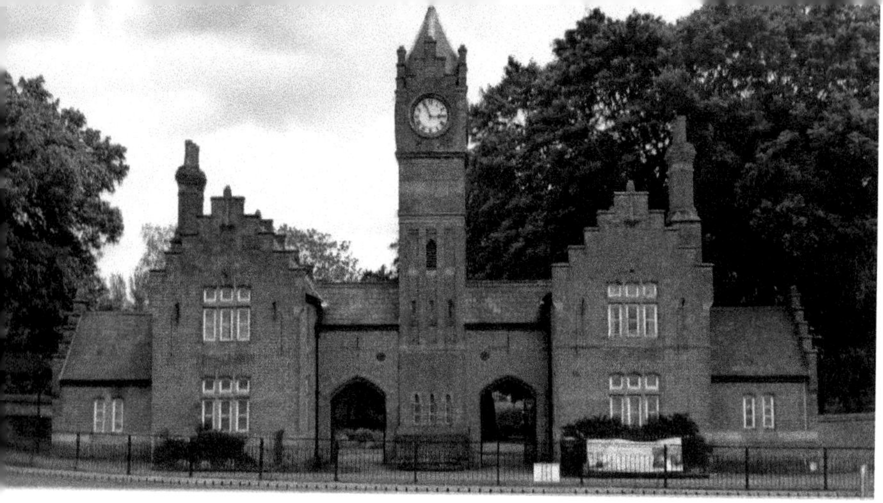

The main gate of Walsall Arboretum.

50. Walsall Arboretum

The Grade II listed Walsall Arboretum occupies the site of Reynold's Hall, the sixteenth-century home of the Persehouse family, developers of lime quarries, limekilns and lime workings.

Walsall Arboretum & Lake Company was formed in 1870 to provide Walsall with its first public park, signing a ninety-nine-year lease in 1873. The park was officially opened on 4 May 1874 by Lady Margaret Hatherton (wife of Lord Hatherton, Edward Richard Littleton), with an admission charge for entry. The site was around 11 acres, with Tudor Gothic-style lodges, two lakes, a boathouse, summerhouses and bandstand, plus space for promenading, dancing, croquet and cricket. In 1881 the park was taken over by the town council on a three-year lease, who introduced free admission. In 1884 the park was purchased from Lord Hatherton for the sum of £4,000, and reopened 21 July 1884 still with free admission. A steam vessel *Lady of the Lake* was launched on the lake in 1878, but in May 1886 heavy rain caused the boat to sink.

Over the years the park was substantially increased in size, and during the First World War was used for growing potatoes and timber, and during the Second World War for allotments.

In 1995 the arboretum received a Charter Mark for the excellence and diversity of services provided.

Walsall Illuminations was a popular annual arboretum attraction held each autumn for six weeks, beginning in 1951. My family used to go every year to marvel at this spectacle, and it was closer than Blackpool! This attraction closed for a time because of lack of funds, and sadly closed permanently after the show in 2008. Illuminations had been an earlier feature of the arboretum from 1875, using candles set in coloured glass jars.

Address: Broadway North, Walsall, WS1 2QB. Tel: 01922 650465.

Postscript

Well that's just about all for now. I hope this book will inspire the reader to visit some, or all of the places I have mentioned. There are other nature reserves within the four Metropolitan Boroughs, so check them out. Enjoy.

Acknowledgements

I would like to thank and acknowledge all the people, individuals and organizations who have helped with the compilation of material for this book, without whom the project could not have been completed.

In particular my wife, Kate, and my son, Peter, for their immense contribution – rewrites, additional facts and proof checking – and to my nieces, Charl and Ali, and my sister, Sioux, for their input. To Naomi Holdstock and Phil Wild for allowing me to reproduce their photographs, and finally to Jenny Stephens, Marcus Pennington and all at Amberley Publishing.

The material for this book has been compiled and assembled from personal research, archive material, various websites and printed matter, and, of course, word of mouth, all of which has been used in good faith. Please forgive me if I have not included any of your particular favourite items.

For further reading I would recommend the works of Bev Parker, Dr John Fletcher, Professor Carl Chinn, and Ian Bott.

A note to visitors of the gems included in this book: not all the gems in this book are visitor attractions; some are not open to visitors but can be viewed in some form from a road or vantage point. Where possible postcodes have been included for those with satnav. Also included where possible is the full address and contact details.

About the Author

Retired managing director John Shipley has lived in Bridgnorth, Shropshire, since emigrating from Wednesbury in the Black Country in 1968, and is now an author and artist. He and his wife, Kate, have two sons and two grandsons.

An ardent season ticket-holding fan of Wolverhampton Wanderers FC, John has had two books published about his beloved Wolves, plus two about Nottingham Forest and one about Aston Villa. He is also the author of four Westerns written under the pen names of Jake Shipley and Jack Matthews. His book *The Little Book of Shropshire* was his first about his adopted county, followed up by three more about Shropshire: *The A-Z of Curious Shropshire*, *Shropshire's Military Heritage*, and *50 Gems of Shropshire. Secret Shrewsbury* was John's fourteenth book to be published and his fourth about Shropshire.

He is currently working on another Western plus a couple of thrillers.

Also by the author

The Little Book of Shropshire
The A–Z of Curious Shropshire
Shropshire's Military Heritage
50 Gems of Shropshire
Secret Shrewsbury
Wolves Against the World: European Nights 1953–1980 (Wolverhampton Wanderers)
Wolverhampton Wanderers Champions 1953/54
Nottingham Forest Champions 1977/78
Aston Villa Champions 1980/81
The Nottingham Forest Miscellany

Writing as Jake Shipley

Montana Skies
Montana Vengeance
Comanche Dawn

Writing as Jack Matthews

Lynching at Prospect Falls